With degrees in hotel management, architecture and inclusive environments, Shivani Gupta is one of India's best-known accessibility consultants. She believes in life and all that it has to offer.

NO LOOKING BACK

A TRUE STORY

SHIVANI GUPTA

RUPA

Published by
Rupa Publications India Pvt. Ltd 2014
7/16, Ansari Road, Daryaganj
New Delhi 110002

Sales centres:
Allahabad Bengaluru Chennai
Hyderabad Jaipur Kathmandu
Kolkata Mumbai

Copyright © Shivani Gupta 2014

ISBN: 978-81-291-2913-0

First impression 2014

10 9 8 7 6 5 4 3 2 1

The moral right of the author has been asserted.

Typeset by Jojy Philip, New Delhi.

Printed at Yash Printographics, Noida

For Vikas

Contents

Prologue

January 2011. As had happened so often in the past, I was torn by conflicting feelings. One half of me wanted to attend the largest college reunion of my batch of 1991 at the Institute of Hotel Management, New Delhi; the other half wanted to flee the city. The last time I had met some of my classmates had been at my wedding, one-and-a-half years ago. So much had changed since then. It was excruciatingly painful to think of putting up a false front of happiness when all I really wanted was to be left alone and to be forgotten.

To have a genuine excuse for staying away from the reunion, I had booked air tickets to Pune for a long holiday with my elder sister, Jiya; but, as luck would have it, I'd had to postpone my trip for professional reasons. Now my dilemma loomed before me, larger than life.

Pushing aside these thoughts, I decided to have a haircut. Once the deed was done, I decided to attend the reunion.

The very thought of going out made me nervy and anxious—I was no longer used to such things, from the perch of a wheelchair. When my friend Sujata called, before she could even say hello, I told her I was coming. It was because of a few friends like her that I was going. It was my way of telling them not to worry, that I was fine.

Since it was going to be a late night, I rested in the afternoon.

Then, as evening approached, I dragged myself out of bed, ransacked my untidy wardrobe and selected a combination of a black polo-necked top and black trousers from a pile of clothes I could no longer fit into. In the past year-and-a-half, I had gained a tremendous amount of weight—not that I was ever slim. But all I did now was eat, watch TV and sleep.

Ritu, my caregiver, helped me get dressed. Vikas had been right in saying that one could never go wrong with black. I threw a yellow-green stole around my neck to add some colour, put some kajal around my dull, tired eyes, used lip-gloss to give a little shine to my dry lips. A spray of perfume, and I was ready to go.

Ritu was going to accompany me to the reunion—I needed assistance in getting in and out of a car. It had become a familiar drill by now. It was nineteen years since I had become disabled, depending on a carer 24x7 to help me with just about everything. Ritu had been with me for nine of those nineteen years and was now more a friend than a paid employee.

That evening, I had decided to take my motorized wheelchair, which made me relatively independent. I had no desire to exhibit my tremendous dependence to my batch mates, many of whom I was meeting after twenty years—friends who had not had the heart to connect with me after I became disabled within ten months of passing out of college.

As we set off for the venue—The Kingdom of Dreams in Gurgaon—a strange feeling of excitement came over me. Maybe it was the name which appealed to me, bereft as I was of dreams now. Sujata was waiting for me at the entrance.

For an instant, I shrank back into the seat. Most of the people standing with Sujata had not seen me before as a disabled person. The boys of my class, now middle-aged men, hastily stepped forward to help me out of the car. One of them offered me his hand, thinking I could use his support to step out, not knowing that I was not able to stand at all. Before I could react, Sujata asked him to let Ritu help me.

In twenty years, I had witnessed all possible reactions to my disability. But this was something new—this feeling of disappointment that they had not been able to help me.

Suddenly, the memories came flooding back.

I'm wondering from where to begin this journey of memory. I guess at the beginning, when I was twenty-two, when I last saw so many of these people gathered around me now, would be a good place.

Book 1

Rebirth

1

Everything seemed so muddled when I opened my eyes. No matter how hard I tried, I couldn't remember saying goodbye to the friends who had come to my house last night for the farewell party I had hosted.

I tried to turn to one side, but I could not. I appeared to be pinned to the bed. Too much trouble, I thought drowsily. I decided to continue lying on my back and closed my eyes again.

Thinking of last night brought a smile to my face.

It had been my last working day, and I was soon going to go abroad to study further. Many of my friends from IHM had come over—this was the first time in the ten months since passing out of college that so many of us were meeting again.

Life in these months had been carefree, and my first job had held little meaning for me. While I may not have had the faintest idea of what was I meant to be doing, one thing I knew for sure—I was not meant to be working at the front office of a five-star hotel. Giving it up was easy. All I really seemed to want, I had realized, was a family—a husband and children, and a life with them.

Yes, last night had been quite a smash hit of a party. Good food and drinks, friends and dance, music… Melodies of Boyz II Men, REM, Gloria Estafan sounded in my head as I saw myself enjoying myself with my friends. I tried moving my feet to the tunes in my mind, but I couldn't. That did not bother me much—the morning after a boisterous party was bound to be like this. Things were good. I had nothing to worry about. And I was looking forward to going to Nigeria for some time and being with Daddy as I decided what was best for me. I slipped into peaceful dreaminess.

✦✦✦

'Chots! Chots! Are you all right?' Latik's voice pierced my ears. Latik was my first cousin and we were housemates in my mother's house as we worked at our first jobs. He was a real sport, so living with him was fun, especially since he fit in easily with my friends. He'd also been at the party last night. He had a sprained ankle and limped through the evening, but this had not prevented him from happily playing his part as bartender.

I panicked momentarily. Was it late already? Had I overslept? But then I remembered that yesterday had been my last working day, so I could sleep as long as I wanted.

When I opened my eyes, I saw Latik standing next my bed. I couldn't recognize the surroundings, though, and unfamiliar sounds caught my attention. I looked at Latik, confused. I was in a hospital, he said to me before I could ask.

I looked at myself. I was lying on my back, covered in a red blanket. There was a dextrose bottle hanging from a stand next to the bed, a tube from it ran towards me.

No wonder! Now I knew why I could not remember either having the dinner that I had cooked for everyone or bidding them farewell.

'Did the party end?' I asked Latik.

'Yes. Everyone has gone home,' he said.

I nodded my head slightly, closed my eyes again and went back to my dream-like thoughts. What had really happened? I must have just passed out. Whatever it was, could not be anything serious—I'd be out of here soon. Besides, being in the hospital would be a new experience for me.

After a while, my mouth felt dry. I asked Latik for water. He put a few spoonfuls of water in my mouth.

'What's happened to me?' I eventually asked.

'We had an accident.'

'An accident!' I finally woke up to the present.

The previous night came back to me in a flash. One of my friends had had a night shift at work. In order to attend the party, she had taken permission from her office to report at midnight instead of ten. Sunil—my boyfriend from college—and I were going to drop her. We were planning to just slip out for half an hour, and I was looking forward to some time alone with Sunil on the way back. But then, somehow, everybody decided to get some air and go along with us. All of us piled into two cars and left. I sat in the front next to Sunil in his car with a couple of other friends in the backseat. The rest, including Latik, were in Kamal's car. Kamal too was a friend from college.

It was late, and to get to the hotel we had to take Ridge Road, which was completely deserted at that time. Both Kamal and Sunil were driving fast. As Sunil overtook Kamal, we all waved at each other, thrilled like little children getting a treat. We were probably touching the 120 kmph mark on the speedometer, just a few moments after overtaking the other car, when everything seemed to spin out of control…

So that wasn't a dream. We had an accident. But…the car hadn't seemed to be *that* out of control…

Everything was so confusing.

'How is everyone else?' I asked.

'Everyone is fine and returned home safely,' Latik said, gently stroking my head.

I felt a certain relief hearing this. I didn't want anyone to get hurt because of my party. I closed my eyes and dozed off again, satisfied that everyone was back home safe.

Latik woke me up again. A doctor was standing next to him, looking down at me. He peered into my eyes with a torch and asked me if I could see well—of course I could see well! He then asked me if I felt any pain anywhere. 'No,' I said.

He then ran his finger along my body, asking if I could feel it.

'Feel what?' I asked, confused. 'No, I don't feel anything.'

The doctor got an oil pin and poked me with it and asked if I felt that.

'Felt what?' I asked, confused again. 'No.'

He lifted my leg and asked me to move it. I couldn't.

For everything he asked, my answer was no. There seemed to be nothing wrong with me. I did not feel any pain, I was breathing normally, my senses seemed all right. The doctor appeared to have no clue about what was wrong with me. He was asking the wrong questions and being useless at diagnosis.

The doctor left with a disappointed look on his face. I knew it was because he could not diagnose anything wrong with me. Before leaving, he asked the nurse next to him to put me on a catheter.

Latik followed the doctor out of the ICU. He returned after a few minutes, looking pale and shaken. I had been diagnosed with a spinal injury, he said.

That meant nothing to me.

My cousin hurriedly said, 'He is just a junior doctor and does not know much. We will know only after the senior doctors come in the morning.' There was nothing to be worried about, he told me.

The following silence was broken by the entry of two nurses loaded with medical paraphernalia. They announced that I had to be catheterized.

I looked at them, puzzled. I didn't know what they meant. All I understood was that it needed privacy and there were no screens in the ICU. Latik got hold of a few people who were sitting next to patients and made them hold up some blankets as a screen around me while the nurses catheterized me.

I asked the nurses what they were doing. They told me that they were inserting a tube into my urinary bladder so that the urine could be emptied out from the bladder.

'What? But I don't want to pee now!' I nearly screamed. I tried to retaliate, but I couldn't move my arms or legs.

This couldn't be happening. It had to be a dream. Everything seemed so out of my control. It was all so strange and embarrassing. I really wanted to wake up. I wanted this dream to end...

❧

I woke up to find Asha Bua, my father's younger sister, sitting next to me. It was reassuring to see her, though there was a worried look on her face. Trying to smooth away the tell-tale lines on her brow, she smiled gently at me and enquired how I was feeling.

'Fine,' I whispered.

She told me that Latik had gone back home to get some

rest and that Naveen Chacha, my father's younger brother, was going to come to the hospital very soon.

I felt bad about putting everybody through this trouble. I was a very independent person and liked to manage my affairs myself. But I couldn't do anything, and Daddy was in Nigeria.

Asha Bua informed me that I had to be shifted to another hospital. They were trying to get me admitted to the All India Institute of Medical Sciences (AIIMS), which was considered to be India's premier government hospital. This hospital was not good enough to take care of someone in my condition.

'What condition?' I asked disinterestedly. As far as I could tell, it was nothing major. And I didn't want to go to another hospital—I was tired. All I wanted was to wake up in the comfort of my own bed in the second-floor barsati in Karol Bagh, where I had lived my entire life.

It was my mother's house, small yet comfortable, made large by my mother's sunny presence and welcoming nature when she was there. No wonder it had become the family house where everybody—my grandparents, uncles, aunts and cousins—would come and stay, especially during the long summer vacations. My mother's personality was reflected in the way she had done up the interiors—stylish, accommodating, warm and simple. She had maintained a lovely terrace garden with flowers, cacti and sometimes even vegetables.

That is where I wanted to go to now, not to some hospital where the doctors would have no idea about what was wrong with me.

Little did I know then what lay in store for me, that my mother's house was to remain only a memory. Unknown to me, my life was hurtling down a path I could never have imagined.

2

It had been nearly nine hours to the accident. My awareness of my surroundings seemed to have improved. I could smell the strong disinfectant and hear the other patients' moans and faint whispers of the people in the hall. But all I could see was the ceiling, my red blanket, the dextrose bottle hanging next to me and Asha Bua in one corner. Smiling at her, I dozed off again.

When I woke up, Naveen Chacha was standing next to me, a gleaming smile on his face. 'Don't worry, beta, we will take care of you. You will be fine,' he said, gently patting my head. His presence and his words soothed me. I was confident that he would ensure that everything went fine. 'We are shifting you to AIIMS. You don't worry, everything has been arranged. You just rest.'

The doctors put a rigid and uncomfortable collar around my neck before discharging me. After I had been carefully transferred to a stretcher, we were ready to leave. Outside the ICU, I saw Sunil's mother and sister coming towards me. I had met them once before, so I recognized them instantly.

Sunil's mother stroked my arm and asked me how I was feeling. I just smiled. His sister, walking along with my stretcher, was telling me not to worry and that everything would be fine. A part of me was happy to see them—it was clearly an indication that they cared—but now was not the time I wanted to meet them, lying on a hospital stretcher.

I was settled in the ambulance with Asha Bua. This was the first time I was in an ambulance. I just lay there, still not sure if this was reality or a dream.

༺✦༻

AIIMS shocked me. I lay on a stretcher for hours in a dirty and overcrowded corridor, along with so many others, in line to get admitted. Pained cries of people waiting to get medical assistance or a hospital bed filled my ears. Patients lay on the floor, not being strong enough to sit up—or perhaps just fed up of waiting to get a hospital room. Flies buzzed around the place and the obnoxiously strong odour of disinfectant overpowered my nose. I wondered if the disinfectant was as effective against germs as it was in subduing all other smells.

It felt like being in hell. I wanted to just get away.

Everyone heaved a sigh of relief when I finally got admission; the wait could have lasted days instead of hours. I was glad—I was going to be on a bed now. I had been lying on the stretcher for many hours and was getting impatient. All the medical personnel at the hospital appeared to come and poke me with an oil pin or tickle me with cotton, asking me if I could feel it, and I was getting very tired of repeating 'No!'

After a CT scan, I was taken to the operation theatre and transferred to the operation table. But I had absolutely no idea why I was there—the doctors had not thought it important to brief me. I was angry, irritated and scared, lying on that table, strong light falling on my face, not knowing what was going to happen next.

I asked the doctor what was he going to do. He told me not to worry and that he was going to fix a skull traction. I did not know what that meant. Before I could ask more, he started shaving my head.

'Why are you shaving my hair?' I screamed. At no cost was I willing to have my hair shaved off. 'Please don't shave my hair!' I cried, begging for mercy. I had always been very conscious about how I looked and worked hard to look good. My hair and its style were an integral part of my appearance. This was not happening, I thought, how could this doctor shave off my lovely hair?

The doctor coolly replied that he was shaving only from the sides and it wouldn't even show.

Shaving only from the sides? That made no sense to me. The doctor was stupid, cruel and unconcerned, I thought. But I also knew that rebellion would not help. I could almost visualize myself, looking like a punk, and I hated the thought of it. While I was still trying to process this, the doctor reappeared with a drill in his hands.

This was going too far. I cowered in terror as he came closer to the table, the drill buzzing.

'What are you going to do with that?' My voice was weak.

Sensing my fear, the doctor said that he had put local anaesthesia and it was not going to hurt—he was going to drill small holes in my skull. The next moment, I could hear the drill buzzing next to my ear, the sound changing as the drill made its way through my scalp and into my skull.

I just lay there, helpless, with my eyes closed. I could feel warm blood oozing down to my ears and tears were rolling down my cheeks. I knew now for sure that this wasn't a dream.

The doctor was whistling a melody from some old Bollywood movie while drilling my head. I was disturbed by this casual attitude. This was the end, I thought, the drill would go through my skull, through my brain, splitting my head open…

❦

Later, I was told that it had been a simple procedure. But how could I have known that then? No one had thought of preparing me for this 'simple procedure' that, in my ignorance, had made me suffer such horror.

After the heavy steel tong was fixed to my skull, I was transferred back to the stretcher and wheeled to my room. My bed was in a four-bedded room, apparently a part of the intensive care unit. But this ICU was noisy and full of relatives of the patients sharing the room with me. The foul disinfectant smell was overpowering here too, but my nose had become accustomed to it by now. It was eight in the evening. The twenty long hours before this, it seemed to me, had been the most harrowing of my life.

It took six people to lift me and lay me flat on my back on the bed. The tong was pulled back so that my neck was completely stretched—bricks weighing about twelve kilograms hung from the tong by a nylon string.

I still did not know the extent of my injuries. I still had no idea what was wrong with me. All I knew was that I would be well soon, that I would be out soon, that life would be back to normal. With these thoughts in my mind, I fell asleep.

3

For some reason, Asha Bua was always there for me whenever something terrible happened. She was someone I knew I could always fall back on—even now, when I was in the hospital with a diagnosis that seemed to worry everyone. It had been the same nearly four years ago, when I was seventeen.

I had just been promoted to the twelfth standard at Welham Girls' School, a residential school in Dehra Dun. Our class went for a trip to Jaipur and Agra as soon as we started our new term. We were to return via Delhi and were going to spend a night in the city before leaving for Dehra Dun the next day. It was a treat for all the Delhi girls as we constantly craved visits home.

Just a week ago, before going for the trip, my mother, who was settled in Delhi while my dad was working in Nigeria, and I, had driven somewhere. I can't quite remember where we had gone, but I remember we were waiting to meet someone. While sitting in the car, we started talking. We talked about a lot of things—school, board exams, future plans, etc. My mother was my best friend and confidante; I never hid anything from her. Out of the blue, she said to me, 'Beta, you must grow up, you are a big girl now.'

I was taken aback to hear her say this, especially when I had become quite independent since going to the hostel. I answered without a second thought: 'Don't worry, Mummy, I can take care of myself. I am a grown-up now.'

On our return trip, the bus was to drop us at the Imperial Hotel in Delhi, from where our parents and guardians were supposed to pick us up. The school bus reached at two in the afternoon. Most parents were already waiting when we reached. My eyes searched eagerly for Mummy, as she would always be on time and never made me wait. To my surprise, she wasn't there.

Within an hour, all the girls had left with their guardians, waving goodbye, happily shouting 'See you tomorrow!' I was the only one left to be collected. My heart was thumping hard by now. I was nervously looking for my mother, checking the various entrances. The teachers who had accompanied us on the trip were also waiting for me to leave. This was strange, not something I could understand. Mummy was far too responsible to leave me stranded like this. I didn't know what to do. I had always been the baby of the family, never having to plan or decide about anything; now, suddenly I needed to do something, to think on my feet.

I called home. Strangely, Buaji, my father's aunt, who lived on the ground floor, picked up the phone. She said in a shaky voice, 'Beta, Mummy cannot go to pick you up, call Asha Bua.'

I was confused, but I did so as I had no other options. My head was spinning with questions. I couldn't understand why Buaji was upstairs. And why was she the one to answer the phone? Where was Mummy? I called Asha Bua and asked her pick me up.

I don't remember having spoken a word to Asha Bua in the autorickshaw on our way home. All my senses were drawn inwards, my mind was racing. Something within me, some kind of a sixth sense, seemed to warn me of something terrible, but I kept pushing it aside. I kept telling myself that the only reason Mummy had not been there to pick me up was because she must have had a severe asthma attack—we were used to her getting an attack sometimes even while we were out shopping; we would just sit somewhere on the roadside with her and wait for it to subside. But the anxiety was killing me.

When the autorickshaw parked outside the gate, I didn't even wait for Asha Bua to finish paying the driver. I ran blindly upstairs and opened the unbolted entrance door. That day, I felt no happy excitement as I walked in through the door; I felt queasy and restless. Our three dogs came running to me as always, except they weren't wagging their tails. I patted them for a moment and walked in.

My face pale, I stared, unblinking, at the sight of my mother lying on the floor, covered by a white sheet. The fragrance of the incense sticks burning next to her filled the room. I just stood there, at the doorway of the room, holding on to the doorknob. My heart was thumping. My stomach was churning, as though the floor was caving in, or I was on some horrible roller-coaster ride.

Buaji was crying. She too had lost the person who took better care of her than anyone else, the person who had integrated a single, middle-aged woman into a family and dispelled her loneliness.

Without uttering a word, I turned and went straight to the kitchen. I started cooking food for the dogs. They had to be fed.

Daddy was in Nigeria and Jiya, my elder sister, was at college in Ahmedabad. Both of them arrived the following day. But on that terrible day, I had to face the numbing experience of my mother's loss alone, with only Asha Bua and other extended family members around me.

Nothing much had changed in my support system in the years after Mummy's death. At the hospital after my accident too, there were only Asha Bua and my extended family members; Jiya was married and settled in Pune and Daddy was still working in Nigeria.

I felt ashamed of myself—a full-grown woman and still troubling my family, despite having promised my mother years ago that I could and would take care of myself.

✳✳✳

I could hear Mummy's voice calling out: 'Time to get ready for school, children. Wake up, Jiya, Chotu!'

As Jiya tossed and turned and finally got out of bed, I moaned, repeating myself for the umpteenth time: 'I don't want to go to school, Mummy, I'll go with you.'

I loved going with my mother to her office in the botany department at Delhi University. School was always my worst nightmare.

Mummy knew only too well how much I detested school. A chatterbox at home, I was a complete contrast in school. An introvert, I never felt comfortable surrounded by other people and so never talked much with anybody—I felt I wasn't smart like the other children at school. Needless to say, I did not make any friends. I was the quietest child in class and always preferred to remain distant from the rest of the students—so much so that my teachers started calling me Queen Victoria, mistaking my aloofness for snobbery. I was much too young to understand what being a snob really meant, so I didn't care much. I paid little attention to classwork and did not get most of what was taught. I lived in my own little world of thoughts wandering around in my head.

At home, though, I was completely different. A carefree child who was always up to pranks. I was never very sporty; instead, I enjoyed being with my elders and trying to con them into giving me goodies. I was very talkative and drove everyone crazy with all I had to say. Asha Bua called me Gappu, someone who is not to be taken seriously. I could not pronounce difficult sounds such as 'ch' and 'sh' and pronounced them as 'n' and 'f' instead. All older my cousins would have a field day with my wrong pronunciation. But I didn't mind them laughing at me. I enjoyed all the attention I got.

Though I loved having my family around, there was only one person I could not manage without—my mother. I always needed the assurance that she was close. When I think back, I do not see anything special that my mother needed to do—she just needed to be around, and that was special enough.

Going to school was like punishment for me, where the best time was returning home after school. From the bus stop I would run all the way home, to be greeted by Ammaji, my great grandmother, and Buaji. They would always wait for me at that time of the day.

Buaji was the one who took care of me during the time my mother was away at work. She helped me change out of my school uniform, and then she would feed me—sometimes with her own hand, especially if there was rice. She would make little balls out of the dal and rice mixed together before putting them in my mouth; I'd gulp it down without chewing properly. She always corrected me, saying 'Chew on your food, beta.' I loved Buaji's cooking even more than my mother's cooking. And she loved me as she would have loved her own child. But while I was generally happy being with Buaji, there was nothing that could distract me from waiting for 5.30 p.m.— that was the time Mummy returned from work. The days she returned early were blissful and special.

Jiya, four years older than me, was my idol—responsible, conscientious and brilliant at everything, while I was a dud at school. I seemed to live in her shadow. All the teachers at school would initially think that I was as intelligent as her, only to realize soon that while she was among the best students in her class, I was among the worst. Jiya returned from school at about three in the afternoon. She would generally pick up the keys to our house from Buaji and go up straight to the second floor.

While Jiya preferred completing her homework upstairs, I'd sit and drink tea with Buaji and wait for Mummy as she always visited Buaji before going up. As soon as the graceful woman with tender dark-brown eyes, a small nose and a warm smile, dressed smartly in a sari, would walk in through the door, I would drop everything and run to hug her.

Though I had no friends at school, I had two at home: Sunaar, the goldsmith who had a shop opposite our house, and Mala, the eunuch who liked to dress as a woman. I suppose I considered them my friends because they didn't judge me, nor I them. I did not need to show them how smart I was for them to accept me as their friend. Mala was a flower seller who sold gajras of jasmine and rose petals out of a basket in the busy Karol Bagh Market. She often visited Sunaar's shop in the afternoon to pass the time. That was where I met her for the first time. She always gifted me a gajra every time I crossed her corner when out shopping with Mummy. Sunaar too often made silver rings and gave them to me as gifts, which I invariably lost. My parents, I found out many years later, quietly paid them for these gifts without telling me they had done so.

I remained an irresponsible and pampered child till I failed in class three. 'Jiya's sister is a failure' seemed to suddenly be the talk of the school. All those teachers who loved me so much, simply because I was Jiya's younger sister, suddenly did not want me in their class. I am sure it must have been very embarrassing for Jiya too. I was so sad the day the results were announced—not for myself but for having let down all the people I loved. I decided to get serious about studies from then on. And I 'improved' enough to become an average student throughout the rest of school.

But that day, as I heard Mummy calling out my name, trying to wake me up, I really did not feel like going to school and continued to plead with her. She had her arms around me, and I cried: 'I don't want to go to school, Mummy, my shoulder is hurting…'

As my eyes flew open to tell her more, Mummy was nowhere to be seen. Instead, before me was Usha Bua, my father's other sister.

'Do you want anything, beta?' I heard her say.

'What time is it?' I asked, needing a few moments to come back to the present and to unshakeable reality.

'It's past midnight. You should sleep, beta. I'm here, don't worry.'

I groaned. 'My shoulder is hurting.'

'The doctor has already given you a painkiller. It'll be fine soon. Just try and sleep.'

I closed my eyes again.

⚔

Mummy had come home early from work that day. I was thrilled. It was one of those days when she purchased movie tickets, and now we were all going to watch a movie.

Mummy would come in and announce: 'Buaji, I've got movie tickets, so get ready quickly.' We generally watched the six-to-nine show and needed to be ready and out within half an hour to make it in time. Hearing her announcement, I'd run up ahead of her to break the news to Jiya. Then all of us, including Buaji, would rush to catch a bus or an autorickshaw to get to the theatre on time. Daddy wouldd joined us at the theatre straight from work. Sitting in the dark hall in between Jiya and Mummy, it would hardly matter that I didn't really understand the story. I loved each moment of being there and waited eagerly for cold drinks and popcorn during the intermission. I would be so happy.

On our way back I would invariably fall asleep in the car. Daddy would then carry me upstairs and tuck me into bed. Daddy was a big and strong man, a 'star' with all the children. He wasn't the one who could manage the children, but he was very good at spoiling them all. My cousins called him 'Wholesale Mama' because he loved to buy goodies for the kids, and that too 'wholesale'. He would buy several kilos of summer fruits, and then sit himself down on the floor to cut and slice them carefully to ensure that the kids could eat them comfortably. When he sliced watermelons, he made sure that each seed was removed before it could so much as interfere with our eating pleasure. My father could not deny his kids anything, but I always was and would remain his 'Little Princess', for whom he had a very special corner in his heart. I thoroughly enjoyed all the affection he showered on me.

That day too, after the movie, Daddy was carrying me up the stairs.

Suddenly, I felt uncomfortable. I moaned and came out of my sleep.

It was morning. There were whispers all around me. Usha Bua, who had been sitting next to me the entire night, peered and asked if I wanted to have tea.

4

It's not easy to drink tea lying flat on your back with a twelve-kilo weight hanging from your head. Usha Bua spooned tea into my mouth carefully, making sure that the temperature of the tea was not so hot as to burn my mouth. After a very long time, I tasted something and actually enjoyed it—I hadn't had anything orally since my accident.

I tried to take in my surroundings. The previous night, I had been too tired to register much. But all I could see well was the white ceiling with water stains in one corner. If I looked down, I could see the white bedsheet and the dextrose bottle on the stand next to me. From the corner of my eyes, I could see Usha Bua sitting on a stool to the right and another patient on a bed to the left. There was a window beyond the other patients' bed.

It was only one day and two nights ago that I had hosted the party. I could remember dancing with Sunil and my other friends. Sunil and I had been together at the hotel management institute and there had been an instant attraction I felt towards him. It was not long before we were involved. He had fine features and lovely long lashes and was probably the first on my list of people that I would consider marrying. Right now, I wanted nothing more than for us to be together as soon as I recovered.

Usha Bua told me that Jiya would be reaching soon and that Daddy would also be here by the day after.

'I'll be fine, ask them not to trouble themselves, Usha Bua.' I didn't like the idea of bothering them. Daddy had just returned to Nigeria a week ago after his yearly vacation and Jiya was so busy trying to settle down in her new business and her marriage. It wouldn't be easy for either of them to come. Besides, I was sure that I would be discharged soon.

Smiling, Usha Bua just nodded and held my hand in hers.

Soon, two nurses appeared to clean with me a bed sponge and change my sheets. This was my first experience with a bed sponge. They pulled some screens around me. I was very conscious about these women seeing my naked body, even if they were nurses. To top it all, the screens had gaps in the corners and anyone could see inside. I kept requesting them to keep me covered with a sheet as I couldn't lift my hands to do so myself, but I doubt if they even heard me. They operated mechanically. After the sponge, they tried changing my sheet. They were not sure how to change the sheet since the doctor had given strict instructions not to turn me. They discussed this for not more than a few seconds and told me they would change the sheets later, after checking the doctor. I smiled and thanked them humbly for their assistance before they marched on to the next bed, taking the screens with them.

This wasn't pleasant. The nurses were careless and rude, unconcerned about another woman's privacy. To me, it felt like a violation of my body; but they seemed blind to this despite being women. It seemed unfair—even if they were doing me a favour by cleaning me when I couldn't do it for myself, as a patient I surely deserved more respect? However, I decided to keep quiet about it—I was dependent on them and didn't want additional trouble for my family.

A team of doctors arrived after a while. They were all men. Looking at them, I thought most of them were probably just starting out in their career. They encircled me, peering down in an inquisitive manner, with a nurse alongside.

'What is the patient's name and age?' one of them asked.

'Shivani Gupta, twenty-two years,' responded the nurse.

'What does the report say?'

'Spinal injury. Spinal compression at C-6/7 level and a hairline fracture at C1.'

They continued to discuss me while I stared up at them, feeling like an object on display that these young doctors would be learning from and experimenting on. I didn't mind it, as I was sure they would tell me by when would I get better and be discharged. Latik, who had replaced Usha Bua, hovered around to get information regarding my condition.

One of them touched the sole of my foot and in reflex my toes moved. There was a sudden surge of excitement among them at seeing this. I was happy too, as it seemed that this was a good sign. They repeated the reflex test several times.

Immediately after this, one of the doctors returned with a piece of cotton and a pin. He tried the same old exercise of poking me and tickling me.

'No, I can't feel that,' was my response even before he asked. Not feeling any touch below my shoulders did not bother me. Having taken the sensation of touch for granted all my life, it did not seem possible that I didn't have it any more—this was a temporary situation, I would be well soon.

Before they left, I asked as charmingly as I could: 'When will I be discharged?'

'Soon, don't worry.'

Latik followed them and returned in a few minutes.

It wasn't even an hour before another team of doctors arrived and we went through the same exercise all over again. Only, this time, Latik very excitedly pointed out to them how my toes moved when my sole was touched. The senior doctor listened to him patiently and tickled my sole himself to verify. 'Hmmm,' was his response, devoid of the excitement the previous team had shown.

❧❦☙

It was evening by the time Jiya reached the hospital. She had come straight from the airport. Even though I had asked Usha Bua to tell her not to come, I was glad and relieved that she had. I wanted so much to hug her, but my arms just didn't move.

Jiya had taken after Mummy and inherited her gentle disposition. She took my hand in hers and kissed my palm softly, saying in her sweet comforting voice, 'Chots, I'll take care of you, don't worry.' We smiled at each other, tears in the corners of our eyes, exchanging our deepest feelings without words.

I asked Jiya to come and stand on the side of my bed so that I could see her clearly. She was wearing a pink salwar suit with white beadwork on the yoke. She had purchased it for me and I had passed it back to her after getting bored of wearing it—we were used to sharing our clothes. Now, she looked worried.

Jiya had always watched over me even as a kid. She was a generous elder sister who always took care of me and also, reluctantly, shared all her friends with me since I found it hard to make friends myself because of self-consciousness. Jiya was a very responsible person even as a child; while I would run around, troubling her throughout the day, she would patiently take care of me whenever Mummy was away—now too, when I was in the hospital, she automatically took over as a mother figure.

The day passed without any talk of my discharge. I had been lying straight on my back for over forty-eight hours, and nobody in the family really understood the prognosis. They simply kept trying to run after the doctors and absorb whatever little information they imparted.

Daddy arrived that night from Nigeria and came straight to the hospital. For the first time in days, I felt truly secure. Daddy had always been there for me, whether it was to buy a dress I had set my heart on or supporting my decision to resign with scant thought of future plans. He was strong and knew how to get things done. I was sure that he would tolerate no delay in getting me out of that dreadful hospital.

But my surge of joy was short-lived. As soon as I saw Meera standing behind Daddy, my bubble of confidence burst.

Meera was Daddy's second wife. They had married seven months after my mother's death, and my sister and I had felt deeply upset when Daddy had revealed his intention to us. His decision came so soon after Mummy's passing that it left us devastated. The sheer urgency demonstrated in the task of finding a suitable companion bewildered his children. After all, it was not as if he was totally unused to being on his own— Daddy and Mummy had been living on different continents for a while, tied to their respective jobs. It had seemed to me that he had just been waiting for Mummy's departure from his life. What hurt me particularly was the fact that the three of us—Daddy, Jiya and I—had had no time to grieve together for our loss and come to terms with it. On the day of Daddy's wedding, I dressed up in a sari and wore high heels to look older than my age. Soon after the ceremony, I packed my bags and walked out of our house and went to my maternal uncle's house. I felt more emotionally secure there; moreover, I could also share my thoughts with Shipra, my cousin sister who was my age. I stayed there for a week, trying to sort things out in my head. Within a year, I had lost my mother, the most precious person in my life; alongside, I had lost the trusting parent-child relationship I had shared with my father. It was my first taste of true loneliness and hardened me from within.

The upside of the painful experience was that I learnt not to depend on anyone except myself and finally emerged from my self-conscious shell. I become an extrovert and gained confidence in myself, as I knew that I had to do it all on my own. There was no one that I could hide behind any more.

Ever since, I had maintained a cordial relationship with Meera. But we took care to see that our paths did not cross much, except during college vacations, when I visited them in Nigeria.

To think that the mere sight of an individual could trigger an avalanche of memories!

Daddy sat next to my bed and held my hand. He took out a packet of vibhuti and applied it on my forehead, arms and limbs. Under Meera's influence, who was an ardent Sai Baba devotee, Daddy too had become equally devout. He kept a small packet of vibhuti under my pillow. 'You'll be fine soon, beta. Baba will take care of you,' he said.

I forced myself to smile. These were not the words I was hoping to hear. I wanted him to say, 'Beta, I'll take care of you always.' I was neither a believer nor a disbeliever. While Daddy had always been religious, I had never heard him talk of God with such total surrender before. A choking sensation filled me. While Daddy's presence was undeniably a reassuring sight, he seemed like a completely different person, without his earlier fighting spirit—he seemed more helpless than anybody else. In his surrender, I felt like I had lost the strength my father had always instilled in me.

5

Days stretched into weeks, but there was no change in my condition. I continued to lie flat on my back, looking at the roof of the ill-kept, dirty hospital room. Occasionally, I'd see a lizard crawling around in my vision zone. These were the sights that had replaced those of my warm home and the grand hotel that I had worked in. Moans and cries of the patients in the adjacent beds had replaced the sound of music and the laughter of friends. My life did not seem mine any more.

The only time that I perked up a little was when there were visitors. They brought with them some of the freshness of the outside world I missed so much.

Sunil visited daily, without fail. Jiya hated him—she held him responsible for the accident—but having him by my side even for short spells gladdened my heart, for everything seemed brighter with him around. Moreover, his presence gave me a sense of purpose to face my situation with a fighting spirit. Somehow, Sunil represented normalcy to me. If he came, it seemed to me, things were not that bad—probably because somewhere deep down I knew that he would vanish if things were not right. It was strange that even after being his girlfriend for three years I didn't really know the person he was; but, I guess, at twenty-two, life is only about what you see on the outside.

Other friends from college visited regularly as well. Of these, one left a deep mark on me. A friend who came to see me was so overwhelmed by my frightful state—the heavy traction and the numerous tubes running in and out of me—that he ran out of the room and vomited. It was a strange experience for me. How could he have had such an adverse reaction on seeing me, one of the smartest girls of my batch? My classmates had elected me class representative in the first year, and I was also elected as the girls' hostel proctor in my third year—how could anyone be so repulsed by me?

Suddenly, I began to question everything—myself, how I looked, just about everything. For the first time since I had landed in hospital, I asked Jiya to get me a mirror.

My hair was unkempt and overgrown. My face appeared the same, except for the dark circles that were more prominent than usual. I looked down at my listless hands—their shape had changed within two weeks. My fingers had curled a little, while my palms were straight and limp. No matter how hard I tried to fold my palms into a fist or straighten my fingers, I couldn't. 'Look at my hands, they look strange,' I said to my sister. Sitting beside me, she assured me that everything would be fine and started regularly moving my fingers and palms so that they got some exercise.

Life had come to a standstill for me and my family. We were all groping in the dark. While others continued to discuss my case with the doctors, Daddy was attending endless prayer meetings for my speedy recovery.

The clock, however, kept its tryst with time, its mechanical ticking reiterating the lack of direction and hope in my life.

I kept my mind away from the daily nitty-gritties that were being managed by my family. I wanted to remain strong for them—they were dedicating each moment of their time and every ounce of their energy in keeping me as comfortable as they could—I could not let their efforts be in vain. I did not know if I felt worse about my physical condition or the agony my family was suffering.

Each new day brought nothing new. Yet, I kept telling myself: 'Tomorrow will be a better day.' I had to hold on to that hope.

But there was no improvement, and the only direction things went was downwards. Because of not being moved or turned, I started developing complications. My stomach stopped digesting any food, so a Ryle's tube was fixed through my nostril—I was now not allowed to take any food or water orally and put on a liquid diet that had to be fed to me through the tube. Even my tablets were crushed and mixed with water and given to me through the tube.

My mouth and throat would get parched and hurt all the time. I would cry for a sip of water to moisten my throat, but all I was allowed was a wet piece of cotton on my lips. In spite of the tube and no oral food, I vomited often. Lying straight on my back made this very difficult; invariably, I soiled the sheet, which was never changed.

I felt as if I had been reduced to just a human body lying on a bed—mindless, thoughtless, emotionless. I had tubes coming out of my nose and bladder, tubes going into my arm, from my head hung bricks, I never changed my position. I was paralysed shoulder downwards and was suffering the onset of a lung infection that was sure to aggravate into a lung collapse.

The doctors had no suggestions to keep this from happening. Rather, they tried to convince my family that this was inevitable—it was as if they were waiting for my condition to deteriorate, having decided that I was not going to improve even if I survived.

A month later, Daddy had to return to Nigeria and to his job. The routine of life had to go on.

❧

While the doctors were promising every day that they would make me stand, they informed my family that the prognosis was poor and that I would now remain and live my life like 'a vegetable'. My family was devastated. Even as they put up a strong front in my presence, they ran from pillar to post to get more information and second opinions. This was in the early nineties, before the days of the Internet, so information was scarce; no one knew much about spinal injuries.

In their frantic search for a more hopeful prognosis, my family found out about a spinal injury centre that was going to be built in Delhi. They went and met the director, Dr Air Marshal Chahal—who, they were informed, was a senior doctor specializing in spinal surgery. He had extensive experience in the armed forces, treating soldiers with spinal cord injuries. The centre was yet to be constructed, but Dr Chahal's team ran a physiotherapy department and a small OPD out of temporary constructed barracks.

My aunt requested the doctor to come and visit me at AIIMS; he agreed. My family took special permission in advance from the hospital administration for him to examine me as an external consultant.

He came the next day, dot on time, exactly at noon. I had expected just another one of the regular doctors with bored expressions who had been coming every day to see me for the past month and a half; instead, in front of me stood a stern old Sikh gentleman. He was tall, fair and lean. His beard was grey and tied neatly around his cheeks and he wore a maroon turban on his head. He looked to be in his late sixties at least and had a very strong personality.

The first thing he said as he entered was: 'Why is she lying on her back?' Jiya informed him that the doctors had said not to move me at all. He was horrified that I had been lying flat for so long, that too on dirty sheets.

As he came closer, Dr Chahal called out for the nurses. They—who rarely visited patients, even after hours of pleading—arrived within seconds. It was his voice and personality—they commanded respect and made people listen to him.

'Come, let's turn her,' he coolly announced to the nurses.

They were shocked, as they were used to not moving me at all. So were Jiya and I. But before anyone could protest, Dr Chahal said gently, 'Don't worry, I'll help you.'

He guided the nurses on how they were to turn me and instructed them to repeat this every two hours. He then asked one of them to massage my back and hips with talcum powder and check if there were any pressure sores. Thankfully, there were none.

This caused a flurry of activity among everyone present in the room—my family, other patients and their families, junior doctors and nurses. There were tears of joy rolling down Jiya and my cheeks—the turning had happened very comfortably, and we were happy just to have this little change in my static situation.

So, after a month and a half, my range of vision changed. I finally saw fully the side of my ward hall and the adjoining bed, things I could see only from the corner of my eyes till now.

The most exciting development was that visually my world expanded. I could finally look out of the window and see the clear blue sky and an occasional bird flying across. I could *see* the things that had been till now only described to me by my family. My day was made, with something as ordinary as turning in my bed.

⁂

Dr Chahal instilled confidence in all of us and gave us hope. He was someone who was willing to look at my injury head-on, unlike the other doctors who had been hiding behind an ambiguous prognosis. We did not require any further proof that Dr Chahal was the doctor I needed.

Once all the commotion was over, he went through my files and said that I should have been operated on immediately after the accident for maximum recovery. Even now, for any recovery, I needed to be operated on in order to release the pressure on my spine and to stabilize it.

Without any hesitation, I took discharge from AIIMS—against medical advice—the next day. I left that horrific place in a private ambulance and headed to the private nursing home where Dr Chahal was going to treat me. The following day, on 1 April 1992, I was operated on. While the world celebrated the foolishness of life, my family and I finally got some sanity back in our lives.

Post-operation, as I gained consciousness, the first thing I noticed was that my head felt much lighter—the skull traction had been removed; my neck had been fixed with a bone graft from my pelvic bone. Though I now wore a rigid collar to avoid any neck movement until the graft was stable, it was a relief to have my head free. I had forgotten what it was to have a head without heavy tongs.

I had lost one and a half precious months only because of the incompetence of doctors. If the operation had been the first medical intervention after the accident, I could have had better chances of recovery and more independence in my life. If only…

In any case, this was a new beginning. I was turned regularly and my sheets were changed every day. Within a day of the operation, my bed was being propped up to bring me into a sitting position. The Ryle's tube was removed and I started eating normal food through my mouth—after a month of being on liquids, it felt like a feast.

One night, shortly after the surgery, while Latik was feeding me dinner, I slowly moved my right hand. After a lot of struggle, I lifted a cucumber slice from the salad plate and put it in my mouth. Latik and I looked at each other, amazed by what I had just done. Then he ran to the reception to call home and let everyone know—this called for a celebration. There was excitement throughout the family that night, and I too felt a sense of achievement, like a child taking its first step. After the weeks of hopelessness, this was a ray of light shining through the darkness. I was not going to be a 'vegetable' after all.

Was everything around me changing, or was I changing? I didn't know the answer to that question, but my goals in life seemed to be shifting as I recovered. My goal was getting discharged and being able to walk; but first I had to focus on smaller goals such as sitting on the bed for an hour at a stretch, holding a rolled chapati in my hand and being able to eat it myself.

All this became possible only after I started understanding my condition. I had long discussions with Dr Chahal about my injury and was made aware of how I was supposed to manage and live with the prognosis. He constantly encouraged me, telling me stories of other people who have done well in life despite being tetraplegics.

With the length of time spent in hospital, my emotional dependence on Sunil seemed to decrease. I started concentrating more on myself and less on worrying about his feelings for me—I was coming to terms with my condition and accepting that things were not going to be the same. In light of my current struggles, his role in my life became smaller. Though he continued to come to the hospital daily, his visit was no longer the only highlight of my day.

After nearly two months, the day arrived when I was going to sit on a wheelchair.

It was not too long ago that I had scorned Daddy's suggestion of a wheelchair; neither was it much longer after the days when I had danced at parties. It is uncanny how, over time, a human being can adjust to and accept his or her changing circumstances. Some time ago, the mere mention of a wheelchair had seemed like a step backwards—today, it represented hope of mobility. Of course, my hopes of walking once again had not diminished but only been deferred. I accepted the wheelchair willingly now because I was tired of being tied to my bed. I wanted to feel the sunshine on me. I wanted to see the people around. I wanted to be a part of the world instead of being secluded. Slowly, I started venturing out of my room.

The day I went out of the hospital building to the porch

is one I cannot forget. Only after getting used to sitting for a considerable time did I try going outside. To face the world, I wanted to look presentable. When I look back on that day now, I see how childish my thinking was, but as I sat on the wheelchair I was sure there was no way anyone could say I could not walk. I wanted it to look as if my sitting on the wheelchair something temporary. The only disappointment was my shapeless hands.

I went out of the hospital entrance with a couple of friends, after nearly three months indoors—it was their presence that gave me confidence to face the world in a wheelchair. I had been a confident, smart and independent person at college—I had a strong mind of my own and did only what pleased me, without being bothered about anyone being with me. But today I was unsure of myself, completely dependent on people around me. There was nothing I could think of doing by myself, not even wheeling my chair in the direction I wanted to go.

I stayed in the nursing home for another month and a half. Like an infant once again, I learnt to sit, to control my bladder and bowel movements all over again. A physiotherapist visited me twice a day to help me strengthen my upper limbs. I had stopped thinking of life ahead by now. There was nothing that I could visualize in my future. There were no aspirations, no ambitions—I needed to relearn simply how to live.

I was fixed, medically speaking, but needed rehabilitation. The only rehabilitation centre that existed in the country in those days was in Pune, part of the military hospital, and I was transferred there from the nursing home in Delhi.

I was happy about this as Jiya and her family were settled in Pune and I would be close to her.

6

While boarding the flight to Pune, I couldn't help but remember the last time I had flown. It had been while returning from Lagos—I had decided to take a short vacation before taking up my first ever job at a Delhi hotel.

I had been travelling alone as I often did. I had been dressed in a fitted royal blue skirt with a white shirt, my hair styled smartly in a short bob, teamed with a pair of my numerous designer stilettoes (my secret weakness)—my appearance was really important to me. I had struggled with my handbag at the Addis Ababa airport, where I had a stopover—the handbag was heavy because of kilos of Swiss chocolates, six pairs of fancy shoes, and make-up and accessories that had not fit in my suitcase—which was filled to bursting with the new wardrobe I had acquired while in Nigeria. (Daddy never stopped me when I splurged.) As I was struggling to carry my bag to the waiting lounge, a tall and handsome man with sharp features had come along and chivalrously offered to help me. A young woman in my early twenties, I had been swept right off my feet just looking at him—how could I refuse the offer he made? I had come a long way from being the quiet introvert of my childhood days.

But this trip to Pune was totally different. What a long way I had travelled from in just a year! Now I wanted to hide and not be noticed by anyone. Clothes and accessories held no attraction any longer as I knew that no matter how hard I tried I'd never look good again. And unlike the occasion of my last flight, I could neither stand nor walk—I was being accompanied by Jiya and Naveen Chacha. My sister and I had discussed each aspect of the travel and worked out solutions. Jiya enquired with the airline and learnt that their ground staff would assist in my embarking in Delhi and disembarking the aircraft in Pune. We were thankful—any assistance was most welcome. Thanks to our careful planning, we managed to reach Pune safely, without incident.

While I was happy to be in Pune, my family was worried that my presence in the city might put too much strain on Jiya. Unacquainted with the ways of life, I could not comprehend how I could be a burden on anyone—forget being a burden on my own sister and her husband, who was an old friend and now family too. That I could be a burden on someone was a new concept that had never crossed my mind before—but I guess society has a way of looking at things that is so rigid that slowly and unknowingly it becomes a part of your own thinking.

༺❦༻

The rehabilitation department was a small part of the huge army hospital complex. Life at the department was regimented and revolved around rigorous physiotherapy. I had always been lazy and never liked any kind of exercise—except dancing— and I still did not appreciate the importance of exercising, when I was relearning to live. But I was given no option. I had to report to the physiotherapy department at ten in the morning and stay there till lunch, and then return for another hour after lunch.

At the centre, I met people who had been living in a wheelchair for as long as twelve to eighteen years. It was then that the permanence of my situation finally hit me. I must have realized this deep down, but I had not been ready to believe it until now, when I was faced with these people. I had no idea how to react to this realization that I was not going to walk again—and I don't think I was even able to imagine the complications and intricacies that came with not being able to walk at all.

Seeing others in conditions similar to mine, or even worse, managing life was reassuring in some ways, I suppose; at another level, though, it was discouraging and heart-breaking. Without conscious thought, my dreams of being able to stand or walk again started to fade. Despite all that had happened, the injury had not touched my soul so far; but now, inevitably, depression crept in.

One day, nearly four months after the accident, while at the physiotherapy department, I saw myself in a full-length mirror. I was bundled in a wheelchair. My back was stooped and I had deep and dark circles around my eyes. My hands had taken on a strange shape, my fingers curling like claws. The hair above my ears, which had been shaved off at AIIMS, hadn't yet grown back; alongside, the rest of my hair had started to fall off because of the trauma and medication, turning me nearly bald. I was pale and thin as a stick. And I could see none of the feminine sensuality that I took so much for granted.

I turned away, horrified, wanting to disown the reflection. Was this what people meant when they used the word disabled? Was this why everyone thought I might be a burden? What was happening to me? *How* had this happened to me?

I had never thought about disability before my accident. Neither had I known anyone who was disabled. Disability had meant social work sessions at school and a feel-good factor from having assisted a disabled person in crossing the road. Disabled for me, until now, had been 'them'. But now...

I think it was that day that I really understood what disability implied. My self-esteem plunged and I became uncomfortable about facing people, aware as I was of the condescending attitude society had towards people with disabilities. I started wearing a scarf on my head when I went out of the ward. I wanted to hide in a cocoon, alienate myself from everybody. This was not me. It couldn't be me.

But then who was I?

More than relearning how to live, it appeared, I needed to rediscover who I was.

> *I changed that day. I changed forever—*
> *I was no longer the carefree person who dreamt of having her own family.*
> *I didn't know yet who I was now; neither did I know how I was supposed to go on.*
> *The one thing I knew was that tomorrow wasn't going to be a better day.*
> *My life from now on was about rediscovering myself—*
> *Struggling to let go of all that I had lost;*
> *Learning to appreciate what I had left.*

BOOK 2

Discovering the Spirit

7

Had someone told me a year ago that an accident could derail life completely, I would have ignored the statement with the casual confidence that is the hallmark of youth. No longer so. In August, I returned from Pune to Delhi and to a life whose contours were frighteningly unknown to me. The city had been like an oven when I left, but its evenings were turning pleasant now. It was exactly six months to the day of the accident, though it seemed like ages.

I was back in Delhi, but all the familiar signposts of my hitherto independent existence had vanished. My mother's second-floor apartment, which had been home for so long, was inaccessible to my wheelchair-bound self; so I was taken to my grandparents' house in Faridabad. They took me in without a demur, though it meant stepping out of their retired existence and back into the whirl of life in their seventies.

My grandparents were a proud couple, fiercely independent. My grandmother suffered from severe arthritis and walked with the support of crutches; but endowed with a hardy temperament, they managed all their affairs themselves. The fact that they welcomed me into their life so readily was heartening, yet the weight pressing down on my heart refused to lift. In my family, love was taken for granted and never demonstrated physically. But now, in my fragile state, I longed to lean against somebody's shoulder and just cry, I longed to be enfolded in a warm hug and be told that I would be taken care of, that everything was going to be all right.

I was relieved to be secluded in my grandparents' house, lurking in the depths of the painful questions and realities that I could not steer away from. There was this stark disconnect between who I used to be and who I was in the process of becoming. My heart said I loved to dance, but my limbs were telling me I could never do so. The pleasure gained from easily catching the attention of men was overlaid by the foreboding that I no longer was and never again would be desirable to men.

Sunil continued to come to meet me on most weekends; I waited eagerly all week for his visit. His presence was the only tangible reminder of all the good times I had had—the carefree attraction, the tingling feeling of first love, the naïve planning for the future...

Both of us knew very well that everything had changed. The accident had taken its toll on Sunil too. He had lost his sunny and light-hearted disposition. In my state of confusion about myself, while one part of me wanted him to leave and find another life, another part wanted to be with him, hoping for a miracle so that things would be good again. At one level, there were concerns regarding my diminishing relationship; at another level, however, I didn't have courage enough to face the world alone.

It was also in August 1992 that I got my first personal carer. Till now, Jiya and Usha Bua had nursed me, but the time had come for them to move on too. It was on 15 August, the day that the entire country was celebrating independence, that I became dependent on my carer, a person who was to become an important part of my life then on. Putul was a young girl from West Bengal. She was going to be my nurse and would also help me in grooming, going to the toilet, sitting, turning, eating... She was not a qualified carer or nurse, but Usha Bua trained her. Much to my relief, she picked up the work quickly and adjusted well with me. It was far more challenging for me to adjust and accept having a personal carer.

It is not easy to accept another person who is to undertake each and every task on your behalf. Being so dependent made me feel extremely obligated to Putul for the services she was rendering. At the same time, there were moments when things didn't go right and I got irritated; but I knew that expressing too much anger might disturb the arrangement adversely, so I would have to retract as soon as I sensed the slightest discomfort in her attitude. I needed my carer to remain happy and comfortable so that she would concentrate on taking care of me and not think about changing jobs. I think having no way out of an unwanted marriage probably feels similar to how I felt about having a carer at that time. I didn't want to trouble Usha Bua and make her train another person, and I definitely didn't want any more trouble for my grandparents. The fear of losing my carer, in the absence of an alternative arrangement, was one that clutched on to me for a long time, often moulding my relationships with others. I was in a precarious situation, so completely dependent on this unknown person, unable to share my predicament with anybody. I often missed Mummy— if only she had been there, she would have taken responsibility for me, and I wouldn't have needed to feel guilty or indebted to everybody.

Having a carer also meant goodbye to the privacy that is usually important to maintain one's sanity. Life with a carer wasn't just a compromise on physical privacy but also emotional privacy—there is little space left for your deeper thoughts with a person constantly with you. Despite everything, however, I also realized that a carer was definitely less demanding on mental independence when compared to family—my carer was the person because of whom I was going to stop being dependent on my relatives and gain enough independence to do whatever little I could.

⚜

Understanding disability itself was not easy. My understanding thus far had been based on what I had seen in the society that I was part of, and I struggled to dispel the images of helplessness it brought. With my first-hand experience, there appeared to be a strong contradiction between what I thought disability was and how I felt as a disabled person. I did require assistance to do things, but I didn't feel completely helpless. In spite of my impairment, there was still a lot I thought I could do. I felt like the same person inside; it was just my physical appearance that made me uncomfortable about facing people. While on the one hand I wanted to hide away, on the other I longed to experience the world after being indoors for so long.

It was ten months after the accident that, for the first time, I felt strong enough to go to the local market with Putul. She pushed me on my manual wheelchair and took me to buy bathing soap. That little task, which for twenty-two-odd years I had taken for granted, now seemed something exhilarating, requiring guts. Having someone push my wheelchair was not a pleasant notion; it seemed to evoke a feeling of pity, symbolizing my dependence—it was not what I wanted for myself. My spirit gave me the courage to step out, but my body made me conscious and tried holding me back. I was nervous about meeting anyone who might recognize me from my walking days. I was sure their questions would make me feel worse about myself.

At the end of the day, however, there was an immense sense of accomplishment and satisfaction I felt in having been outside and faced the world. I couldn't compare it with any other achievement in my past. It wasn't so difficult after all, I thought. Of course, the stares of strangers made me squirm; but if I was able to ignore that, it wasn't so bad. I could no longer enter the shop on my wheelchair since it had two steps, and I had to learn to be satisfied with just sitting outside while my carer shopped for me. But I didn't mind that—adjustment and acceptance were my mantra. In my own eyes, I was a winner, and my award was the soap bar I had purchased. Excitedly, I told my grandmother to tell me to buy whatever she needed from the local stores rather than troubling my grandfather. There was finally something I could do for them.

It was these small pleasures, which to others may seem frivolous, that made me persevere. It was the accumulation of countless such little achievements over a long period of time that helped me to convince myself that my inabilities were not reflective of me; rather, it was all my abilities that defined me. I had embarked on a journey to get better. The final destination was not known to me, but what was exciting was the journey itself. While the prognosis for how independent I might become physically was not good, these small successes allowed me to never look at only how bad the situation was. They made me concentrate on what I could do to make my situation better. I had truly started living for the day.

Outwardly, my body looked weak. But internally, I felt stronger, taking charge for the first time in my life. It was difficult to fit myself into the picture of a disabled person painted by society. I was determined to draw a line between my physical condition and my spirit, which seemed so much stronger than my body.

Often, people asked me how I felt about the accident. Did I feel angry? How did I feel about all the sudden changes that the accident had brought with it? I did not really know the answers to those questions. I had lost everything familiar, and as a beggar for a better future, anger seemed pointless. I was far too involved in living each day. Each day was a challenge, with several ups and downs. Each day was like a lifetime of learning and experiencing. I had pondered enough about all that I had lost without any results; it was time to move on. In the mist of soul-shaking sadness, anger had no place. Moreover, there wasn't anybody I could express my anger to!

Sunil remained an unclosed chapter in my life for several years. As time passed, we seemed to lose touch gradually—me, struggling every day; him, progressing in his life and work. It was strange that, even though we hardly ever met and I was sure I had no place in his life any longer, he seemed to be the one I wanted. He brought hope. It was to be good enough for him that I thought I was ready to believe in miracles and go forward. It is only now when I look back that I am able to understand that it wasn't him that gave me hope but what he represented to me: a man who was once attracted to me, a light at the end of the tunnel. News of his marriage to someone else more than five years after the accident didn't come as a surprise to me. In fact, it freed me from the false castles I had built in the air.

8

It was sometime in early 1993 that something as ordinary as a box of six small poster paint bottles, gifted by a friend, gave me some direction in life. My friend told me that she had struggled hard to think of what would be the best gift for me. She wanted something that wouldn't hurt my feelings, so she had crossed out clothes and shoes. She also wanted to buy me something I would use, which made her decide against books and make-up. After careful elimination, she had decided on the paint box. She was unaware, though, that the paint box was representative of all that had changed since then. I thanked her with a smile, but the gift brought back memories of my time at the Institute of Hotel Management, when I had basked in the glory of my paintings.

Soon after joining college, I had been called to the principal's office. The principal remembered me from my entrance interview, when I had talked about painting being my hobby— painting was really not my hobby, but for entrance interviews one has to say things just for the sake of it. He asked me to paint two oil canvases for the college. Paint two canvases! It was an unheard-of request made from the principal to a student. I couldn't believe it—the principal had taken me seriously while I had unthinkingly rattled off something during the interview. He didn't want to see any of my previous work, a portfolio or even a photograph of any of my previous work. He just went ahead and told me to paint two canvases. I was nervous about taking on the responsibility—I had had art as a subject for my board exams, but that did not qualify me as an artist! But I was more nervous about refusing because I thought it would create a bad impression of me right at the beginning of college life. Stuck, I decided to give the paintings a shot—and I succeeded! Even today, after more than two decades, my painting has a place in the principal's office.

Those were the days when failure did not seem like a possibility...and now failure seemed to be the only possibility. I took the paint box, but in reality it seemed useless since I couldn't even hold the brush in my hands. It kept slipping out. Aimless and empty as my days were, struggling to dab just a few strokes of paint on paper filled my time and brought some colour into my drab existence. Without any concern for how it turned out, I continued trying to paint daily, almost mechanically. It was a frustrating experience as, very often, I would accidentally drop the paint. At other times, the brush would slip, spattering the paper with unwanted strokes. I discarded sheet after sheet of paper without producing a single painting that I was satisfied with. But it hardly mattered. Nothing that was happening was great. So how did it matter if my paintings were not great either? There wasn't anybody judging my work, and it was good exercise for my hands.

After more than a year of the accident, I still wasn't able to write properly. I had to use my thumb impression instead of signing while closing my bank account. Although the doctors had assured me that I would be able to write again, the thumb impression came with its own package of self-doubt. But thanks to all the painting practice, even though I never regained the ability to hold a pen or a brush normally as everyone else does, I learnt an alternate way of holding my brush to get better control over it, and I was able to improve my writing too by holding my pen in the same way. In time, painting became more than a hand exercise for me. It became a way for me to pour out all my feelings on paper through the brilliant colours. Whether good or bad, painting was the only constructive thing I was able to do at the time, so I spent most of my time on it. After days and weeks of practice, and after discarding numerous sheets of paper, the dabs finally started taking some form.

One of the first things I did with my awkward-looking paintings was to fold them into thank-you cards and post them to everybody in my family, people who had so selflessly been there for me. I was indebted to everyone for taking such good care of me and the only way I could repay them was by working on and improving my condition. Their love, care and genuine concern could not be repaid by material gifts.

A neighbour who was studying at a Delhi University college had a brainwave one day. While chatting with me, she excitedly said, 'Hey, why don't we sell your hand-painted cards at our college fair?'

I looked blankly at her and, a little embarrassed, said very softly, 'No one is going to spend a penny on my cards, they are not worth buying.'

In spite of her insistence, I closed the discussion. I knew that my cards were precious for me but not worth spending money on for others. Before leaving, however, my neighbour took a couple of cards from me, saying that she wanted to give them to her friends.

A couple of days later, she returned and said that all the girls in her college had loved the cards and that the fair organization committee really wanted me to put up a table displaying and selling my cards.

My heart skipped a beat on hearing this. I cannot say whether it was because of excitement or nervousness. I couldn't believe my ears. In that one moment, countless thoughts passed through my mind. Why should anybody want to buy my cards? How was I going to face everyone there after being homebound for nearly two years? I was aware of the feelings my appearance evoked in people's minds—would I be able to accept their pity? What if things went wrong? Would I be able to manage?

It seemed easier—and safer—to simply put her off and forget about it; it was far more difficult to take on the challenge. Agreeing to go was just the beginning. What was more difficult was planning the trip, the biggest hurdle being my incontinence and my inability to use regular restrooms. Besides, how was I going to travel to the college and back?

I had not yet worked out a simple way to transfer into a vehicle. I needed two to three people to get me in and out of a car. And I did not have the courage to hire a taxi and go on my own. Whether I could attend the fair or not now boiled down to my transportation—if that worked out, I could go. My options were pretty much non-existent as all public transport was inaccessible. Till that day, I had not thought that transport could become such an important issue in my life that it could capsize all my plans. Finally, Swati said that she would drive me to her college in her father's car. She would pick me up from home, where we would get help to transfer me into the car; once at the college, her friends would help get me out. My grandparents too encouraged me to participate, and it was all decided.

The programme brought a flurry of activity in my mundane and static life. We were to go to the fete on Sunday, and I worked hard day and night and got about 150 cards ready to take with me. I was very excited and thought constantly of how it was going to be. After a long time, I actually thought about what clothes I would wear. In these months, it hadn't mattered how I looked as I never really went out except to the local shops. Now, suddenly, there was concern about looking presentable in a crowd of young women. Dressing up seemed sacrilegious somehow—as a disabled person who could no longer connect with her femininity, I felt I had no right to be putting on make-up or looking stylish.

Then there were the apprehensions about managing my incontinence. My bladder was trained to void every three hours to avoid accidents. But the trip to the fete and back would take at least six hours. I was used to going to my uncle's takeaway, but that happened within the three hours; I needed to remain dry for double the time. This was a big challenge. I stopped drinking liquids from Saturday evening itself. I told myself that without 'input' there would not be any 'output'. I was prepared to starve myself to participate in the fete. It was not easy to deny myself liquids when I was thirsty, but this was a price I needed to pay to avoid accidents. Thankfully, it was winter, so I expected to manage without much difficulty.

We left from home early Sunday morning. It was a cold day, so I wore a long skirt with a heavy sweater. I wasn't at all happy with my attire, but this was the best I could manage. I had changed so much. Once upon a time, I was a person who loved dressing up. But today I was worried about what people would think seeing a disabled person like me dolled up rather than actually enjoying dressing up. I had had to let go of all my nice dresses, high-heeled shoes and other accessories, but this was of no significance to me any more. It didn't matter how I dressed any longer because, in any case, all people saw was my disability. I wanted to look as ordinary as possible and merge into the crowd. I wanted to be absolutely unnoticeable. I was probably as conscious of myself as an adolescent girl is when thrust into a group of new people.

As I set up my table at the fair, I was a bundle of nerves. How would people react to me? I was full of apprehension about being there. As the girls started trickling in, a few came to my table and casually looked at the cards. I sat behind the table, alert, observing them carefully to get some feedback from their expressions and their chatter. I was seeking answers for whether they pitied me for sitting in a wheelchair or disliked my cards. I was hoping to know more about myself from them. Of course, I got no clues—there was only a sense of indifference that came through. This, paradoxically, reassured me that I merged in and was not sticking out like a sore thumb.

Some of my concerns about my new status as a disabled person were dispelled that day. I had myself made the whole issue larger than life, I realized—when it came to people outside the family, no one was really bothered about me. I was also thrilled at the way the girls reacted to my cards. They loved them, and all the cards sold like hot cakes. I made lots of money—at least, in my terms. I was happy that I had agreed to take this opportunity and challenged myself to go to that fete. To get out from the comfort of home in the situation I was in then needed a lot of courage. The fact that today I am easily able to travel around the world is probably all due to the gutsiness I had mustered that day.

Apart from being fun and making me some money, that day

restored to me some of my former confidence. As I look back today, I know that I had laid the foundation for an independent future on that cold winter Sunday.

9

It wasn't long after this that Daddy returned from Nigeria for good and I moved in with him at our house in Patparganj in East Delhi. It had been two years since my accident, and also almost two years after which I was meeting my father. Until now, Jiya, my grandparents and my extended family had looked me after, and I wasn't really sure how I felt about being with Daddy after having learnt to internalize my pain, disappointment and despair. The worst was over, so Daddy's return did not actually signify much to me. The joy and meaning of being with him seemed to have vanished over time. All it meant now was that here onwards Daddy was going to take care of me instead of my grandparents; otherwise, my life was going to remain the same.

The good thing that I could clearly see, though, was that with Daddy's return my grandparents, who had done far more for me than their age allowed, could be freed from responsibility. Also, I was back in Delhi—and that surely meant more opportunities for me, especially since I felt more confident about facing the world again.

Daddy, I felt, had his own reasons for returning to India, though he said it was to take care of me—he would prove the truth of this with his actions in the years to come. I was his priority, beginning with ensuring that I was comfortably settled in the new house as soon as possible. Meera visited off and on, staying at times for only a couple of days. She remained busy in her own world, in her own house, taking care of her mother while Daddy, prematurely retired, devoted his energies to taking care of me.

The first thing that we did as a family after Daddy's return was go for a road trip to Haridwar for blessings. It was a trip that taught me a lot and moulded my thinking in many ways.

While I was in the queue to enter the temple at Haridwar, a poor middle-aged woman from the village walked up to me and handed me a twenty-five paise coin. I was sitting casually dressed in a nice T-shirt and trousers, and I looked up at her confused. Why was she giving me money? My instinctive reaction was to fumble out: 'No, no! This is not mine.' I thought that she imagined I had dropped the coin and was returning it. But before other words could come out of my mouth, the woman had left.

For several moments, I just sat there, looking at the coin in my hand and the lady walking away. It took time for my brain to analyse what had just happened. This was something that had never happened to me before, and I had not imagined that it would ever happen—she had thought that I was a beggar!

The only thing that distinguished me from everyone else there was my using a wheelchair. The woman had thought me a beggar simply because I was disabled! She had assumed that because I was disabled I was needy. I did not know how to react—whether to laugh at her naiveté, or feel sad about what I had been reduced to. With her one little 'charitable' act, the woman had managed to make me question my own being.

I laughed off the incident, deciding to keep the coin as a reminder of this bizarre encounter. In reality, however, that was a defining moment of my life. It was a reaffirmation of what I had always been aware and conscious of—that people judged me on my outward appearance alone. No one seemed to have the time or inclination to get to know me as a person, with my own strengths and weaknesses, just like anybody else. Providing me with charity was probably much easier than to try and really understand what I needed.

As I look back today, after two decades, I still see the same charity being distributed in so many different ways to people with disabilities. So much so that most governmental programmes for people with disabilities revolve around concessions and reservations—that is far easier to offer instead of creating a enabling environment and equal opportunities that would allow them to nurture their abilities and become equal members of society.

It was the condescending behaviour of society towards disabled people that made me angry, more than the fact that I was severely disabled now. I could learn to handle and overcome all the problems my disability brought with it, but there was no way I could change society's attitude towards me. In my long struggle to find myself, there were always instances similar to this that pulled me down, chaining me back within the house and forcing me to feel sorry for myself.

That one incident made me recognize fully the need and importance for me to be self-reliant; I could not depend on others' goodwill. I had always been taken care of by my family and never needed to be self-sufficient, but the taste of charity was so bitter that it was not something I wanted to experience ever again. Economic dependence on anybody meant that I needed to have that person support my decisions. But I was not content to have to seek approval for my every action from someone else. I wanted to someday become completely independent—and the only way to do so was to take responsibility for myself and stop relying on anybody for anything. Everyone had looked after me adequately, but I did not want to be a burden any longer. I had to find a way to be self-reliant.

My head full of these thoughts, I tied a holy thread at the temple in Haridwar, with a fervent wish to God to make me independent. But I doubted very much even then that any wish made to God was going to be fulfilled without putting in my best to achieve it. I needed to find my own opportunities and create a path for myself.

10

Life was a paradox. While on the one hand there was greater understanding of independence, on the other hand Daddy very willingly and lovingly looked after me and took all responsibility for me on his shoulders. He represented me everywhere, did my thinking for me, supported me and fought for me—there was nothing I had to do myself. He took complete care of everything, without my needing to worry about anything. I really appreciated all that he did for me; but, at the same time, I craved to experience the big bad world for myself. Strange as it may sound, I wanted to make my own mistakes and find my own successes—as any other person would at the age of twenty-four.

But there were other challenges that awaited my attention. Taking on the next one proved far more difficult than I could have imagined.

For me, Daddy had always been the caring person who would apply vapour rub on his body and make me sleep next to him when I suffered from bronchitis as a child simply because I didn't like the burning sensation the rub caused on my own skin. But now he suddenly seemed to become someone who couldn't understand the importance of a personal carer for me. There was always discord in the house as he constantly found fault with Putul. At times, he was unreasonable in his thinking—he said that I cared about her more than I cared about him. I was crushed by this. I could not understand how a person who was so gentle to me could be so harsh to someone else. It was very hard for me to maintain a balance between my love for my father and my anger at his irrationality.

At that time, I was deeply upset about the circumstances and unable to comprehend why Daddy was so ruthless with my carer; but now, when I look back, I tend to believe that somewhere in his heart Daddy was angry about witnessing my helplessness. Until I started living with him, he had only heard about my situation; now he could not bear to see me needing so much help. He wanted me to be the same again. He wanted to enjoy the hot cup of tea that I used to make for him, which he loved. He wanted to continue pretending that I could pull him up to a sitting position when he was lying down by simply pulling on his little finger. The carer symbolized my inabilities and the changed circumstances that he was struggling to accept.

I was caught in a strange dilemma. The more Daddy vented at my carer, the more I wanted to break free—I wanted to move out and build my own home. The more Daddy helped me with my matters, the fiercer became my desire to be independent—I wanted to be my own boss and make my own decisions.

I continued to paint and kept myself busy with it, trying to escape from reality. With Daddy taking care of everything, things were up to date and very well-managed, although the discord with Putul continued. Immersed in painting, I built a fortress around myself—where I was alone with my colours, oblivious of everyone around me, lost in myself. I painted for about ten to twelve hours a day, talking and arguing with myself, singing and crying, thinking and planning my future. It was therapeutic in many ways. Most importantly, it helped me voice my thoughts, even if nobody was listening.

I had no social life, and I was isolated amongst my own people, with whom sharing my deepest concerns was difficult considering the unnecessary discord around me.

Acceptance back into society after becoming disabled was next to impossible. I had already tried getting a job in the back office of the hotel I used to work at before my accident, but my disability got the better of me. After this rejection in the field I was trained for, and at a place where I had already served, I knew that getting a job anywhere else was not going to be easy. This rejection was yet another clear indication of the fact that I would now need to restart my life from the scratch and retrain another skill—my hotel management degree was not going to be of any use to me any longer.

In this situation, painting somehow seemed to become my new profession. In a day, I painted as many as fifty cards. All of them were pictures of delicate, translucent flowers that I copied from the numerous books and photographs Daddy pulled out—being an agriculturist, he had quite a collection. I laughingly call myself a card-making machine. In time, with more exposure and encouragement, I gained greater confidence about facing the world and displaying my paintings. Knowing that I had to become self-reliant gave me the strength and determination to push myself beyond my limits.

Painting brought some meaning back to my life and helped in healing my self-worth. The hurt I felt each time people sympathized with me was mitigated when someone appreciated my work, my talent and my ability. Besides, painting gave me an identity. Often, one is judged by what one does. And painting gave me an answer to the question 'What do you do?' I was a budding artist!

❦

Within a very short span of time, I changed drastically as a person. From being nervous and self-conscious about going to a college fair, I had turned into someone who took up each opportunity to sell the hand-painted cards, mostly at various fairs. Charitable organizations were my best contacts and they gave me more opportunities to sell. Some of them were monthly fairs and my cards became very popular. I went to at least two fairs in a month and made some money.

Participating in these fairs month after month and selling cards from a little table was the only way of earning I knew now. I often thought about all my college friends, who were by now holding good positions and had promising futures. Some of them had even married. And here I was, selling hand-painted cards, making not more than Rs 3,000 a month, four years after passing out from college. But no matter what, I was happy to be doing something productive and remunerative, and it consumed every ounce of my energy. As I look back today, I wonder why I never felt belittled selling my cards. I think it was only because I was far too committed to becoming self-reliant. My goal was so clear that I did not mind starting from the bottom of the ladder once again. It would have been far easier for me to give up then and be dependent on Daddy for the rest of my life, but it was a challenge to exert myself day after day, climbing ahead one step at a time, and I truly enjoyed it.

Earning Rs 3,000 wasn't easy at all. I travelled in an autorickshaw to sell my cards. Travelling in an auto for a tetraplegic with a wheelchair and a personal carer was reckless and next to impossible—yet, I did so because that was the cheapest mode of transport available to me. Travelling by bus was not feasible because there was no way I could board the bus in my wheelchair. Getting into an auto was not easy either, but it is rightly said that 'Necessity is the mother of invention'— with a lot of thought and effort, I worked out a way. I would request the auto driver to lift me with the help of my carer and then transfer me into the rickshaw seat. Once in the auto, I sat in one corner where the fixed metal rod prevented me from falling out. The wheelchair was then folded and put in next to me, helping to hold my legs in position. My carer would then swing herself into the auto.

One thing that was predictable each time I went out was the recommendation of a 'miracle cure' available in some village or the other. Most often, I was told of these cures by the auto drivers; and if not the driver, then definitely some person on the road. I could not blame people for sharing these recommendations because a disabled person is generally viewed as someone needing treatment to become 'normal'. What all these people failed to understand, however, was that I wasn't ill in any way and that I considered my wheelchair merely as a mobility aid as I could no longer walk—I was not using the equipment because I was unwell. I learnt to think of those incidents as amusing rather than irritating and trained myself to laugh at them. I am sure I knew about all the 'miracle healers' in India during those days.

Not a penny of my earnings was spent on extravagances—I hadn't been out shopping for clothes or accessories even once after the accident. My money went towards my transport and buying more materials for painting. How I had changed from being a girl for whom her salary meant little, her pocket money far exceeding what she earned! Now, I did not want to take money from Daddy. Whether this change was a result of growing up or being disabled or the process of truly recognizing myself, I do not know. I was satisfied that at least I didn't need to ask my father for extra money for my painting materials. It was a small step towards complete self-reliance.

What worked well for me at these fairs was that I got the opportunity to meet a number of interesting and influential people, some of whom I met every month. Sometimes I also met journalists at these fairs—they thought that I made for a good story of 'grit' and 'survival' for the newspapers. It was also through these fairs that I got the opportunity to have a solo exhibition for my paintings. I had displayed my work in several group exhibitions by now, but this was my big chance. My work was to be exhibited within a management school premises in Delhi. I could hardly believe it—all my perseverance and hard work seemed to be paying off after all.

My interaction and phone calls with Jiya had dwindled since Daddy had returned. With Daddy's return, she was assured I that was being taken care of—so responsibility for me had taken a backseat for her. She was also busy taking care of her daughter Ira, who was now about two years old. During this time, she hardly ever came to Delhi as her business, home and daughter kept her hands full. But when she heard that I was going to have a solo exhibition, she could not help going overboard. She immediately started work on designing a brochure of my artwork. Even though she could not attend the exhibition, her gift of several copies of beautifully printed coloured brochures and visiting cards, with a flower as my logo, reached me well before the exhibition.

The excitement of having a solo exhibition made me work day and night. With the brochures, it now seemed a very professional affair and not an amateur exhibition, and I was determined to put it together as best as I could. The big day arrived in May 1995. A well-respected person, who owned a big business empire, inaugurated the exhibition and purchased a couple of paintings right away. The gallery was full of friends and invitees and people came up to me and congratulated me, some of them complimenting me on my watercolours.

It a spectacular feeling—that I was being appreciated for my work, for my abilities. I had proved to the world that my abilities exceeded my disability.

There were media people too at the exhibition. One of them was from a television channel and I was interviewed for a spot on TV; the print media folk made notes about what I had to say. I felt like a star that day. For once, I didn't care about being disabled. The exhibition was a grand success, and I sold quite a few of my works. I was happy to have managed to achieve this.

Following the exhibition, there were articles in all the leading newspapers about how 'The Flower Girl' who could not hold a brush properly in her hand created delicate watercolour paintings. They were stories about grit more than art, meant to inspire readers. I was content with the success of my exhibition, despite my uneasiness about the media making out my paintings to be some kind of superhuman act that required a lot of courage. I was uneasy because anyone putting up an exhibition needs to work hard for it—and here I was, getting so much attention solely because I was disabled. However, publicity was new to me and it made me feel known and important. I decided to enjoy the limelight, brushing aside my qualms.

11

It was in early 1996 that my life finally got some real and stable direction. Vikram Dutt, who had counselled my family in the initial days of my injury, when they were given to believe that I would always remain a 'vegetable', came to visit me at home. He was the one who had introduced my family to Dr Chahal and was a board member of the upcoming spinal centre. He was a warm well-built, middle-aged Bengali gentleman. He spoke very eloquently and had a way with words.

He asked me a question I had not thought about in depth till now. He asked me what I wanted to do in the future—continue painting, study a subject which could get me a regular job, or work in rehabilitation helping people with spinal injuries?

The future. I had just been following the direction life seemed to be taking. I hadn't even realized that there were so many options available to me to choose from. Yet, it didn't take me more than a second to respond. 'I would like to work in rehabilitation if given an opportunity,' I said seriously.

In spite of all the laurels and recognition I had gained from painting, I knew that it was not what I wanted to pursue as a profession. The reason being that it didn't seem like a very stable profession, and I could never judge if people purchased my paintings because they really liked them or out of charity towards a disabled artist. Knowing this was crucial for me. All the media stories about the budding 'disabled' artist made it difficult to differentiate my talent from my disability. I didn't want to base my life on charity. I would be happier painting only as a hobby, where I didn't feel the pressure to sell my work.

Studying further to get a job seemed like a faraway, unachievable dream. There were many difficult questions that I had no answers for. What would I study? Would I be able to manage, having never been serious about studies before? How would I go to college, given the practical problems of transportation, inaccessible college infrastructure, my need for a personal carer to be with me all the time, and so on? And, finally, there was no guarantee that I would get a job even after studying further—having already been rejected once because of my disability.

I knew that in choosing to work in rehabilitation, I could contribute the maximum. And being disabled myself, there would always be a place for me in the profession. I was confident that I had made the right choice. Destiny was unfolding itself to me, and Mr Dutt was the catalyst to help me get to the next stage of my life.

Mr Dutt told us that he could organize a two-month training for me in the UK to be a 'peer counsellor', if I was interested. As a peer counsellor, I would be required to help people struggling with spinal cord injuries to come to terms with their condition. I thought it was the ideal role for me. It was an opportunity for me to make a real contribution by offering information and support to spinal injury survivors. This was exactly what was lacking at the time I had my accident, when my entire family was groping in the dark, aching to know more from doctors who were far too busy to discuss anything. If I could help in plugging that gap, then there would be nothing better I could do with myself. Moreover, there would be no charity or sympathy involved in my work as I would be working with other people with similar suffering.

* * *

I left with Daddy for the training on 1 April 1996. It was exactly four years after the day I was operated on. At Heathrow Airport, a taxi booked to take us to Salisbury in Cornwall picked us up. I was to be trained at the Duke of Cornwall Spinal Treatment Centre for a month and a half. We were put up at the hospital staff accommodation. The rehabilitation centre was about a ten-minute walk away, in the same campus.

A visit to a developed nation such as the UK was good for me in many ways, even aside from the training schedule. While I had been to other countries in Europe before, this experience was just not the same. Now, as a disabled person, there was a sea of difference in how I perceived everything. While earlier I'd just notice the beauty, architecture or the cleanliness of a place, now there were many other aspects that I was absorbing— including the way disabled people interacted with their environs and how society responded to their needs. The idea that the country appeared responsive and accommodating to its disabled population was new—I was used to a society that cared very little about its disabled and it was up to them and their families to make do.

The first thing that I noticed as soon as we drove through the Salisbury town centre and towards the hospital was the number of people using wheelchairs who were out and about, going on with life in the most regular manner. Not all of these people were disabled; a number of them were elderly. In India, one is not used to seeing disabled people out on roads. Most of them remain cooped up in their homes. But here the presence of people with disabilities everywhere seemed something not out of the ordinary.

Each time I went out in Delhi, I was used to bystanders being curious about what had happened to me and feeling sorry for me and saying 'Chhi chhi! See, such a young and pretty girl in a wheelchair—who will marry her now?' Such remarks made me feel sad for myself for a while. But as I got used to hearing them, I would think: 'Yeah, I know I cannot get married... but who wants to get married anyway?' There were numerous instances wherein I was told off at offices—they said I should not have troubled myself to visit personally, I should have sent a representative. My physical presence to them seemed like a burden. I often wondered how that would have worked, given that I wanted to be self-reliant, do my own work and become part of mainstream society. Seeing all the disabled people doing their chores themselves in Salisbury confirmed to me that my feelings were justified.

I was impressed by the systematic and organized way in which rehabilitation happened. Unlike me, who was self-rehabilitated because of inadequate expertise and support availability. The most important learning for me from this trip was the realization that disability was not the end of the road; rather, it was just an obstacle to be overcome through rehabilitation. It was in Salisbury that I understood the true meaning of rehabilitation. I also understood disability a little better—that being disabled wasn't a big deal. All the patients at the rehabilitation centre projected an attitude of being regular people who happened to be using a wheelchair. There was not an ounce of sympathy or charity that their demeanour invited. It was amazing to be there—an absolute eye-opener.

One of the most memorable events that I happened to attend while at the rehab centre was a cocktail party organized for all the current and ex-patients of the centre. I can never forget that evening. Laura, who was an ex-patient and now also my friend, came to pick me up at seven in the evening—in spite of being a paraplegic, she drove herself and also managed to load her wheelchair into the car. This was a party where I was going to go alone, without Daddy. I was nervous about how I was going to manage, yet I was very excited at the thought of having a social evening without my family. Laura assured me that there would be many paramedics attending the party and they would be able to assist me. Off we went in her car.

The party was taking place in a large indoor basketball court at a local school a couple of miles from the hospital. As we reached and were preparing to get out of the car, true to the English weather, it started raining cats and dogs. We waited for a while, but since knew it was not going to stop raining, we decided to get off and make a dash. One of the paramedics helped me get into my chair; I was expected to be able to wheel myself to the hall from the parking area. I remember struggling on my monstrously heavy Indian steel wheelchair which refused to budge, while Laura zipped off on her lightweight wheelchair. But I was determined that I was going to make it. I was not ready to exhibit my dependence. I wheeled hard on the steel rims, slippery from becoming wet. By the time I reached the hall, I was exhausted. But waiting for me inside was an amazing experience.

The hall was filled with people. The only difference from

a regular party setting was that more than half of the guests were people in wheelchairs. There were more than fifty wheelchair-users in that hall, each one of them enjoying the pulsating dance music and the drinks. There were a number of people swaying in their wheelchairs to the music along with their non-disabled partners. For someone like me—who missed being able to dance more than she missed walking—this was a pleasant surprise. After my accident, I think I had in some ways become unknowingly rigid. I had thought that dancing to music was no longer for me as I couldn't stand. But that evening, seeing people enjoying themselves so freely, unshackled me from my apprehensions. The mood was so light and gay that I just sat there for a few minutes, my eyes wide with awe. Was this possible?

I was recalled from my thoughts by Laura asking what I wanted to drink. Since my accident, all I drank was non-alcoholic drinks, but I did not want to feel out of place at a cocktail party. 'I don't know,' I told her, 'I'll drink whatever you're drinking.' I got a glass of beer a couple of minutes later and sat with Laura and her friends, drinking.

'Guess what? Andy proposed to Nina just before you came in,' said one of the people we were with. There were shrieks of excitement from the group. 'That's lovely!' said Laura in a singsong way, clapping her hands.

Once the excitement subsided, I asked Laura, 'Who is Andy?'

'Don't you know him? He is admitted at the rehab centre. Andrew—I'm sure you've met him.'

'Oh! That Andrew? He's got engaged?' I had met the guy in question. I was soon lost in thought. How could he be getting engaged while he was still in a wheelchair? And that too, in the hospital, getting rehabilitated?

'He is engaged to Nina, his therapist,' Laura said after a few moments. 'You must know Nina too.'

Of course I knew Nina, the pretty physiotherapist. Why would she want to marry Andrew of all people, I wondered. Sure, he was good-looking—but he was also a paraplegic.

'Look at them, they look so lovely together.' Laura pointed towards a couple on the dance floor.

Nina and Andrew had apparently met in the hospital and fallen in love during his rehabilitation. It was beyond my comprehension—a non-disabled person falling in love with a disabled person! Yet, they looked so lovely together. Nina sat on Andy's lap quite comfortably, and he was holding her in his arms. They were hugging and kissing. They seemed so much in love that it was like something out of a fairytale. Was this really possible, I wondered the entire evening, gazing at them with a sense of envy.

12

On my return from the UK, I got a job at the Indian Spinal Injuries Centre in Delhi. The centre had finally started taking shape, and I was going to be working under Mr Dutt. I was thrilled to be offered a job there not only because I would be employed and have a regular source of income but also because I would now be a part of an institution that would make a difference to the lives of people like me. I felt I had been given an opportunity to repay a bit of all that I had received from my loving family and well-wishers.

The centre was located in Vasant Kunj, at the other end of town from Patparganj. To travel daily an up-and-down distance of almost sixty kilometres was not going to be possible for me. The management kindly offered me a room on campus. Since the staff accommodation had not been built yet, the room was in the sheds that were acting as a temporary construction office while the building was coming up. It was extremely rundown and not really in a state of occupation. But the option of living there was better than travelling daily.

If anyone asked me 'Is the accommodation safe?' my response would have been 'No, not at all!' The room was located in one corner of the campus, right next to the boundary wall, and was far away from the guardroom. My carer, Putul, and I were the only two twenty-four-hour occupants. After work hours, the place became completely secluded. All the staff left for home by five in the evening as the hospital was not functional. But I was not scared. I owned nothing worth stealing.

If anyone asked me 'Is the accommodation comfortable?' my response would again have been 'No, not at all!' Initially, the place did not have a kitchen. With the hospital kitchen too not functional yet, I had to order my meals daily from a local takeaway. My room was small, with an asbestos roof that heated up like a furnace during the day. Even basic amenities like a telephone, television or a refrigerator, which one usually took for granted, were not there. The toilet was not attached; I had to get out in the open and be pushed to the toilet. This was particularly embarrassing when I had to shower as I used the bed to dress and undress. The route till the hospital was un-tarred and would become unusable for me during the monsoons.

But if one asked me 'Are you happy to have shifted?' my response would have been 'Yes! I am elated.' There was nothing better that I could have asked for and nothing more that I wanted. I felt like I was one of the luckiest people alive.

It was, without doubt, a reckless decision for me to live there, being a tetraplegic. But it was precisely then that I realized that I liked being reckless. It was a challenge to manage living there, but the challenge was what made life worth living.

I was moving out from under my family's wings. I was going to be independent. I was ready to fly.

Therein lay the irony. Before the accident, all I had wanted was to be loved by my family, and to find a man I could fall in love with and marry, thus extending this circle of warmth. Carving an independent identity was never on my list of to-dos. The accident, I came to understand, had changed so much more than my physical appearance—it had changed everything. After four years of being taken care of, I wanted to get away from the warmth and security of my family—nothing seemed more important than my quest for self-reliance.

From someone who wanted to be completely dependent on her family, I had become someone who decided to live away from her family because she wanted to be independent. I knew that my family's concern and care for me would always inhibit my independence. I had compromised enough because of my disability—I didn't want to make any more compromises. I wanted to live on my own terms, take risks and carve out my own identity.

There was another important reason for me to move out of Daddy's place. Daddy loved me dearly and would do anything for me, but this meant adjustments for all of us—Daddy, Meera and for me. Each of us had our weaknesses, and these were not always acceptable for the others. My greatest 'weakness', if I may call it so, was the need for a personal carer. This was not easy for Daddy to accept. It was clear to me that my moving out was the best way to retain a good and peaceful relationship for us. Besides, ensuring that I wasn't being a burden on Daddy obsessed me—making me not do half the things I wanted to experience. Failures and disappointments were going to be a part of life for me, but I didn't want Daddy to go through them. And I didn't want him to keep fighting for me, trying to protect me. I had to learn to fight my own battles and make my own life. I was best off being on my own.

It was time for me to take off.

I started my job with a lot of enthusiasm and put a lot of hard work in it. From being someone who spent hours behind a table painting, I was now someone who could be spotted zipping around the hospital premises on my new and stylish lightweight manual wheelchair purchased in the UK. There were suddenly many new people around me, and I was excited about getting to know all my colleagues.

I was, simply put, too happy. I was happy to have achieved something for myself and be out of the family cocoon. I was happy to be starting my life again. And, as with all beginnings, there was excitement about the future. The sky was my limit.

Since there were no inpatients when I joined and I could not do any peer counselling, I was involved in other tasks. One task that I took upon myself was compiling fact sheets on various aspects of spinal injury. I called the booklet 'All your questions about a spinal injury answered'. It was meant for patients and their families so that they could understand the problems they may face after a spinal injury, and it also explained the issues of long-term care in simple words. It was a one-of-a-kind booklet in India. These fact sheets were so appreciated that work commenced to translate them into Hindi. Many years later, the centre printed them after some edits and sold them in the hospital for all the inpatients. However small, I was happy that I was able to make some real contribution. It was simple information like this that my family and I had so missed receiving four years ago.

It was nearly two years after I joined that the centre started getting inpatients. In those two years, I worked as part of a team that was involved with an internationally funded research project. One of the tasks we undertook was to raise awareness about spinal cord injury amongst medical and paramedical staff all around India. Spinal injury was an unknown quantity in India in those days, with just a handful professionals working in the field. With the high numbers of patients with this kind of injury, it was important to raise awareness and create platforms for discussion. After all, if only I had got a more knowledgeable doctor at AIIMS, I could have probably been far more independent than I was able to be. There was so much work to be done—whatever we managed to do was just a drop in the ocean.

The team at the centre comprised young professionals—all of them starting out in life, full of energy and with many fresh ideas. I was able to gel easily with the rehabilitation team. I went home on most weekends, but my life revolved around my work, the horrible accommodation I lived in and the new friends I was making. I was also glad that I didn't need to run to Daddy for every little thing and was able to manage my own affairs. As a disabled person, I knew that life was all about adjusting to the society around me and I had been accustomed to foregoing many things just because I did not want to trouble my family any more than what was minimally needed. But now I was living in my own little world, not worried about causing trouble to anyone. This came closest to leading a regular everyday life like everybody else.

While I continued my struggle to just be a part of society, Daddy continued to fight the legal case that was filed at the 'Motor Accident Tribunal' against the car insurance company for compensation for my disability caused in the accident. It took six years to resolve. Daddy fought it patiently and diligently. Any other person would have got tired and frustrated and would have settled out of court, but not him. He believed that we had a genuine case that needed to be heard and settled in the right way. He wanted to ensure that his daughter was compensated for all that she had lost in her life.

Just a week before the compensation case was decided, Daddy told me about the holy ash that was falling from all the pictures of Sai Baba displayed throughout the house. When I visited home I was, in fact, surprised to see the ash sticking to the pictures in big lumps. It did indeed seem like the ash was oozing out of the picture, but I did not know what to think. I believed in it because of Daddy's belief. The holy ash was a sign of blessing for Daddy—he had fought the case tooth and nail till the very end and it was well worth it.

I received a landmark judgment, with a sum of rupees twenty-four lakhs being awarded as compensation. It was the highest ever granted in those days for the loss of limbs. Having some money safe in the bank gave me a certain sense of security. Suddenly, there was also the possibility of exploring things I had not thought about till now.

❦

I started peer counselling once the centre had inpatients. I concentrated on working with women, the reason being that they had the same physiology as me. As well, the hospital management thought that a female counsellor for women and a male counsellor for men was the appropriate way forward.

Spinal injury is known to be one of the most traumatic injuries recorded. I knew first-hand that acceptance of the injury is probably a lifelong process. So I didn't expect these women with fresh injuries to be able to even comprehend the life changes that were still to come their way, while they were in rehabilitation and not yet discharged into the real world.

What was good was their reception to what I had to tell them. Their willingness to understand the injury was far greater when the information came from me rather than anyone else because they knew that I was talking from experience and not only theoretical knowledge.

As a peer counsellor, I tried to remain detached from their personal problems—though I could see clearly how each one of them seemed to be going through the same emotions and experiences I had done, and I could see their families struggling in a manner similar to mine. But I knew that the struggle and the pain were inevitable. It was all part and parcel of adjusting to the situation.

I tried to explain spinal injuries in four ways to them. First, I tried to make them understand what a spinal injury really is, and all the complications that come as a package with it—issues such as incontinence, high risks of pressure sores and urinary infections, respiratory dysfunctions, etc.

Secondly, I explained the life-changing habits they needed to inculcate to be able to live a healthier and fulfilled life. Things such as the minimum amount of fluid they must drink, the kinds of food to eat and to avoid, or even simply protecting themselves from excessive heat and cold to avoid falling ill.

Thirdly, I tried giving them hope by citing examples of people who had succeeded in living life successfully in spite of spinal injuries. But though I talked about such success stories with the patients, at a personal level I could never draw inspiration from other people with spinal injuries who had continued to live a full life—I knew that there was hardly any such option available to me. I drew inspiration from the people around me who touched my life. I also drew courage from thinking about people in harder circumstances than mine, disability being irrelevant, who continued to live life no matter what. At times, I even drew inspiration from the very patients I counselled. The fighting spirit in people, the struggle to exist and the determination to continue—that was what really touched my soul.

As the fourth and final step, I talked to the patients about issues relating to settling back in with their families. It is not as easy as it might seem because, with a spinal injury, one no longer holds the same position in the family, no matter how selfless and caring one's relatives are. This was probably the most difficult for me to talk about because I myself was, in a way, trying to run away from my own family and friends. I was, after all, searching for myself and my identity away from my family. I knew the people who once thought me clever and smart now felt sorry for me—the only way I could handle this pity was by staying away.

There were a number of women from varying economic backgrounds that I had the opportunity to meet during this time. Some women, who were already married, were worried about how would they manage to take care of their husbands and families, and some of them were nervous about their husbands abandoning them. Those who were unmarried never broached this topic as they all hoped to get well someday and find a man. The biggest challenge that almost each woman faced was to accept herself now as a 'care receiver', while she had earlier been accustomed to the role of 'care provider' within the family.

In the fears of these women, I seemed to relive my own fears over and over again. The only thing that I had wanted out of life before my accident was to find a caring husband and children—this simple dream was shattered the day I looked at myself in the mirror at the rehabilitation centre in Pune. If I myself could not accept my changed physical form, how could I expect anyone else to?

I don't know how far I was able to really help the various women I counselled, but I definitely gained a lot from them. Each one was unique in her circumstances, and how she worked her way through those circumstances was unique too. Each one of them was a champion in my eyes. It didn't matter if they couldn't perform activities as easily as they could before the accident, it didn't matter whether they were able to earn money or look after their family the way they had before. What made them champions was that they continued to fight no matter how hopeless the future seemed. After all, I knew very well how difficult it was to continue the struggle day after day and how tempting it was to give up and simply say 'I can't'.

Sanam and Richa were two young women I interacted with during that time. Both belonged to middle-class families. One had been injured in a car accident, the other owing to an accidental gunshot. They were both some years younger than me and both continued fighting through their problems, despite the many ups and downs. Today, when I look at them, I feel happy. Sanam runs a pet boarding centre along with her husband and Richa works at a software company. They are now smart and confident women, and there isn't anything they cannot achieve.

As for me, the balance sheet I had maintained in my mind since the accident now looked like this:

What I lost
I had lost a lot.

There was the pain of being left behind, while everyone progressed.

I had to restart my life, while everyone else I knew continued to build theirs.

I struggled for very basic thing like managing my bladder and keeping my carer humoured, while everyone else fought greater and more important battles in their lives.

What I gained

I had gained as much as I had lost.

I learnt to gain happiness from small achievements, while others didn't have time to feel happy.

I had found success in the number of people I was able to give hope to, while others measured it in their salaries and designations.

I felt satisfied with whatever I had, while others failed to find satisfaction even with everything at their disposal.

13

My new friends at the spinal centre were all therapists from the rehabilitation department. They were all at least five years younger than me and had just graduated from their colleges. I could no longer relate to people my age and I connected much better with these young people. The fact that they were starting off at their first jobs resonated with my situation of working at my first job after becoming disabled. All of us had big dreams for our future and a long way to go. With energy high, we worked hard and enjoyed ourselves just as hard. Lunch hour used to be the best, when all of us shared our lunch. The rest of the day we worked.

One of my closest friends during the early days of working at the spinal centre was Annie. She was a fresh physiotherapy graduate when she joined the spinal centre. She was from Bhubaneswar, and a confident young girl with delicate features. She was a simple person who always dressed in plain salwar kameezes and had a very gentle soul. A patient, it seemed to me, would probably heal just from being in her company. Her father accompanied her when she came to join—since there was no staff accommodation available at the centre, she was trying to find a place to stay near the hospital.

Putul had got married by the time Annie joined. This had brought a new set of challenges for me as I had to be alone at night. Putul would put me in bed by nine in the evening and come by seven in the morning to get me ready for work. It wasn't easy for me to continue like this, but I had no options. I used to regulate my water consumption and stop drinking by seven in the evening just so that I didn't need to pee during the night. Since I needed help to turn in bed at night, now that I was alone, there was no way I could do that. Through trial and error, I learnt to sleep the entire night on my stomach. That way, I was the least prone to bed sores.

Because I had no carer at night, my evenings had begun to look like this:

Dinner: latest 7 p.m.
Last drop of fluid intake: 7 p.m.
Last trip to the toilet: 8.30 p.m.
Settle in bed on stomach: 9 p.m.
Turning in bed at night: never.

It was frustrating when, in spite of such a regulated routine, I had incontinence accidents some nights. And there was one night when there was an infestation of big black ants all around my stomach and groin; I realized this only in the morning when Putul came and turned me as I lacked any sensation. I lay sleepless through countless nights, worried about something like my toe being twisted and me not being able to put it right, or consumed by some hissing sound that I was sure was a snake. Still, it was okay with me—it was a test of my limits, and a small price to pay for my independence.

When I heard that Annie was looking for accommodation, it seemed like a good idea to have her bunk with me. Not that it would change my regimented routine, but it would still be nice to have someone around for emergencies and I would sleep better. Annie was quite willing to share the room as that would put an end to her paying-guest-accommodation hunting and she would be on campus. Our sharing the room was not only good for both of us in practical terms but also resulted in a great friendship.

It was not long before we started having a lot of fun together. Annie was one of my few friends for whom my disability did not outweigh me—she enjoyed being my friend regardless of my disability. She asked me not to worry about being alone at night and said that she would take care of me. And she did so. For her, my disability was not a problem or a burden—it was my friendship she valued and I, as a person, was more important to her than my condition. The two of us went out often, sometimes for dinner or for movies. During these times, pushing my wheelchair out on the road or helping me transfer into an autorickshaw never bothered her.

Once, the two of us, along with another colleague, went to watch *Titanic* at Delhi's first multiplex cinema theatre, owned by Priya Village Roadshow Ltd. This was my first time at the newly built multiplex, and I had no idea about its accessibility. Upon reaching, we were informed that a wheelchair user could access only two of the four halls. Thankfully for us, *Titanic* was running in one of the accessible halls. Once in the hall, we realized that I would need to sit separately in one corner while my friends sat somewhere else. It seemed that accessibility of the hall for the multiplex management meant a person using a wheelchair could enter the hall and park in the aisle in a corner, irrespective of being accompanied by other people. The whole point of watching a movie together with friends was defeated. I sat alone through the movie, fretting and fuming over this treatment—after all, I had paid the full ticket price.

By the time the movie was over, I was shaking with anger for being singled out and treated in this discriminatory manner. On our way out, I made it a point to bring this poor service to the notice of the management. Screaming at their manager at that time felt really good. It helped me vent my anger and cooled me down. I also wrote a long note in the complaint register, knowing full well that it was a waste of time. By the time we reached home, I had forgotten the whole incident. In any case, there was nothing more that I expected. Living in India, I was used to having all my complaints ignored. But it appeared that I was wrong this time.

I was surprised when, a couple of days later, I got a call from the senior manager of the hall, saying that he wanted to come and meet me. I gave him my office address and asked him to come during my lunch break. He came, and in his hands were the most beautiful bouquet of powder-pink lilies and white roses that I had ever seen and a box of chocolate truffle pastries. He handed these over to me, along with a handwritten personal apology letter from the owner of theatre chain. I looked at him, stunned for a moment, and then with an ear-to-ear smile accepted the apology. He promised that their management would look into issues of improving accessibility for disabled people and left after chatting with me for a while.

I was happy to have received the lovely gifts with the apology letter—it was a gesture far beyond my expectations. I felt like a winner because my voice had been heard and someone had taken notice of the problems I faced. Voicing my discomfort to the right people did help after all, I realized. For a couple of days after that, I went around bragging about the apology I had received and showing off my bouquet to everyone. The theatre management invited me once again to their halls to suggest inputs for improvements. I suggested quite a few; unfortunately, hardly any were implemented. Even today, after more than a decade, the multiplex remains the same—their excuse being that they are in leased premises and therefore cannot make changes.

It was having a friend like Annie that had given me the courage to fight at that time. Unfortunately for me—but, of course, good for her—Annie left after working for two years. She returned to Bhubaneswar, where she was to soon marry a childhood friend and then continue to work in her own city. I was going to miss her. Though I had made a number of new friends, there was no one like her.

Suddenly, after two years, I was back to living my cautiously regimented life.

14

It was in the summer of 1997 that I met Vikas for the first time. He was studying to be an occupational therapist at the National Institute for the Orthopaedically Handicapped (NIOH) in Kolkata and was in Delhi for his summer vacations. He had come to my office at the spinal centre with a message for Mr Dutt from one of his professors. I was to take the message as Mr Dutt was not available at the time.

I was working at my computer when Vikas walked in and announced: 'I want to meet Shivani.'

Hearing my name, I turned around. 'Yes, I am Shivani. How can I help you?'

Little did I know then that I was facing the man who was going to change my life forever, that he would become my best friend, lover, comrade and guide. How was I to know then that I was looking at the man who was going to become the reason for me to live? I had no idea that I was looking at my soul mate.

Vikas was an attractive young man. He had thick, black, curly hair that was very striking against his fair complexion. His most prominent features were his eyes. They sparkled with life and boyish charm.

Vikas gave me the message and was out of the room in ten minutes—and so were any thoughts of him from my mind.

But a year after completing his degree, Vikas joined the spinal centre as an occupational therapist. He was twenty-two then.

He was filled with all the energy and freeness of spirit that characterizes any person of that age—the same age at which I met with my accident. Life at that age, I knew from experience, was always carefree, with the future just beginning to unfold. Vikas was no different—except that his love for life could not compare with that of anyone else I knew.

Vikas hadn't liked me at all the first time we had met, I discovered. He had thought me very high-handed. And truly, at that first meeting, he had been just another person for me. But after he joined, we started getting to know each other a little. We mostly met during the lunch breaks, when Vikas loved to eat out of everyone's lunch boxes since he hated carrying his own. With his charming personality, he quickly became popular, particularly with the girls. Some of them even started getting extra food especially for him. He came across as very friendly, and the smile on his face never seemed to fade. Everybody found him attractive and very approachable. He was sharp and witty, with strong points of view. He did not easily agree with the crowd, though he got along with them. He was gregarious and talkative, but his choice of friends was very well defined. He was someone who would go all out for his friends and expected the same in return. What I liked most about him was his great sense of humour.

One day, during the lunch break, when all the patients had left the department for the wards, we sat around the table in the physiotherapy department to eat our lunch. Out of the blue, talk about a road trip to Nainital and Ranikhet came up. And instantly it was decided that we would all pool in together, hire a vehicle and go for the trip. I had never been to Nainital, so without thinking too much I joined in the discussion excitedly. I agreed to pay for two shares, one for me and one for my carer. I had not been on a road trip with friends after becoming disabled, so I didn't really know how it would work out. But since I was going to be with friends, I knew I had nothing to be scared about.

We went for only two nights, so there was little time to spend at any one destination. But still I enjoyed the trip very much. It was a big new step for me to go on an outstation holiday with friends. The challenge of being out on my own made it even more enjoyable—it was a test to see if I could be out with friends for a long time without them having to be worried about me or my comfort. I'd say I managed very well, except at Nainital. The rooms we got there were on the first floor, so I had to be carried. But everything else was good. As a tetraplegic with a number of special needs, to stay two nights in uncomfortable, cheap, inaccessible hotels without many amenities was a piece of cake after living in the horrible hospital accommodation.

Everyone in the group enjoyed trekking, except for Vikas and me. All of them went off excitedly to trek once we reached Ranikhet, leaving the two of us behind. Even though they called us spoilsports, we didn't care much. We decided to have our own fun and share drinks until everyone returned. That was the first time that Vikas and I really talked about anything serious. Until then, it had all been jokes and pranks. I guess both of us got to know each other quite a bit that evening. We enjoyed each other's company and, strangely, seemed to share a lot of interests. We spent the entire evening chatting like old friends catching up with each other after a long time.

Vikas belonged to a middle-class Punjabi family settled in Delhi, I discovered. He had a brother who was four years younger than him. His parents were hardworking people in government jobs and had raised both their children with love and care. Like in most Indian families, Vikas too had a very close-knit circle of uncles, aunts and cousins he had played with as a child. His childhood, it seemed to me, was very similar to mine. The only difference was that while he continued to be wrapped in the love and security of his family even now, I was struggling alone. Vikas had always been a day scholar and lived at home throughout his schooling. Staying in a hostel during college was a big change for him since he was very attached to his parents. During 'ragging season'—the first few weeks of college marked by the rites of initiation, usually in the form of mild (or, in the case of medical colleges, sometimes quite severe) torture inflicted by the seniors on the freshers—Vikas had actually run away from college to the shelter of his parents' home.

Vikas was always brilliant at studies, so not having good attendance in classes had no effect on his results. While at school, the only way he would study was by making his mother read out all his textbooks and listening to her, he told me. In college, he did well by borrowing class notes from girls who were more attentive and up to date with their work. He would further condense their notes, make his own and then breeze to the top position. He was extremely popular in his college and had a lot of friends. In Delhi too, he seemed to have a big circle of friends and spoke of them with great affection.

As I told him about my life and my struggle to move

forward after becoming disabled, Vikas's eyes became larger and sparkled even brighter—he was like a child listening to his favourite story. He was strongly affected by the struggle I had put in to reach where I was. I had met a number of people who appreciated me for my strength, but no one had had a reaction like his. He sat there for several moments, speechless and staring at me. He kept repeating: 'Wow, Shivani, you're a hero!' He said that he had never in his life met another woman like me and admired my strength. That was the only time he said this in front of me—never again, in all the years we were together, did he appreciate me to my face!

While I was happy to have made a profound impression on Vikas, I wasn't sure about his reaction. I wasn't looking for this kind of appreciation from him or from anybody. He seemed to be in awe of my achievements, while I never thought of any of my actions as great achievements. All I wanted was to try to continue living like anyone else, to be a part of society. I could not help but point out to the childlike young man—so impressed by me that he had instantly put me on a pedestal!— just how protected a life he had led till now, without having to be worried about anything. I even mocked him a bit, saying condescendingly, 'You don't really know what life is.'

One quality of Vikas that I couldn't see that day and only understood over time was that while on the one hand he had a very childlike and sprightly disposition, on the other hand he was a most mature and radical being, someone who could stick to his principles and not take things for granted. I had assumed then that I had found some excellent friends on the Nainital trip; it was much later, after the trip, that I got to know that none of them had really wanted to take me along because I was disabled and was going to be accompanied by my carer—with the two of us, their fun would have been hampered. It was Vikas who had put his foot down, saying that if they had asked me and I had agreed to go, then they better take me, else he wouldn't go either. He put his foot down not because he was any great friend of mine—we hardly knew each other before the trip—but because he felt it was unjust to leave me behind after having asked me. He would have done the same for any other person in my position.

I was, of course, heartbroken when I learnt of the hypocrisy of people I thought were my friends. It seemed my disability outweighed me even in the eyes of my colleagues who worked with me to help other disabled people. But it wasn't something I could blame them for—they had merely reacted in the manner they had been taught by society. It was an experience that influenced my future life to a very large extent.

I realized that it was better for me to remain in my own space, where people could come to me, rather than encroaching into anyone else's space. That way, they wouldn't need to make any 'special' arrangements for me—and everyone remained happy. Then onwards, I developed a habit of inviting people over to my place rather than going out with them. Even today, there are only a handful of friends whose homes I have visited. I am always more comfortable with them coming to meet me.

I also learnt the difference between 'good-time' friends and real friends. Both Vikas and I had several good-time friends throughout the time we were together, but it was just us—each for the other—when it came to real friends. We stood by each other, sharing our lives with each other.

Most importantly, I identified the limits that I should remain within when it came to people who seemed to always expect me to adjust or understand if things excluded me or were not up to my expectations. As a disabled person, if my friends exclude me from taking me along for a rock show, a movie or a pub, then I am supposed to understand their difficulty and let go rather than expect them as friends to assist and ensure my inclusion.

This incident left a mark not only on me but also on Vikas's mind. He was unable to appreciate this discrimination towards a friend because of disability and seemed to be able to empathize with me without my uttering a single word about my dejection to him. The incident resulted in triggering a much closer friendship between us.

15

When I look back at that time, I tend to be astonished at myself. I am amazed by the resilience, acceptance and will to go on that I had during that time. I bet if I tried living in an accommodation like that even for a day now, I would fail. It was the importance I gave to managing to live on my own, to getting to know myself better and to trying and becoming a part of society, that pushed me onwards.

Since there was no way I could afford to live elsewhere, I didn't really talk to anybody about the challenges I was facing while trying to be a part of society—spending my nights alone without a carer, and the rundown state of the accommodation. Thankfully, none of my family members enquired in detail about how I was managing. But my headstrong attitude did take a toll on my body. I was hospitalized three times in three years and was on a ventilator twice. It was the recurrent hospitalization that raised the alarm and became the reason for the decision to shift to a better and cleaner accommodation. I did not have the courage to take such a big decision on my own, I felt, and needed the approval and support of my father and other family members.

It was a big decision for all of us. There seemed to be so many pros to continuing living on the spinal centre campus— the most important being that it was easy for me to get medical attention. Another advantage was that, though the accommodation was dreadful, it was part of the institution and was like living in a hostel accommodation. Living in a rented flat, even if it was close to work, would mean that I would need to take on much more responsibility. But then everybody realized that it was time for me to step into this next stage of life, no matter how difficult it might seem.

Finding rented accommodations with the number of special conditions that I required was not easy. I needed a ground-floor flat for sure, and it needed to be within walking distance from the spinal centre as there was no way I could depend on using public transport every day. And, as if this was not enough, I was a single and disabled woman wanting to rent a flat. This was not a good prospect for would-be landlords. After a tiring wild-goose chase, we found an apartment only because the spinal centre agreed to give me a company lease. Daddy, of course, did all the running around on my behalf. I know that without his support at that time, it would not have been possible for me to do what I did. Even though I was twenty-eight, because of the time I had spent away from mainstream society, I had lost my worldliness—I was as naive as someone in their early twenties.

Finally, the day to shift out of the rundown barracks came and I moved into my new place. To express in words how happy I was is difficult. There's no place like home—what an apt phrase! And who could appreciate this phrase better than me? All through the trying years after my accident, I was provided for and looked after by Jiya, my grandparents, my uncles and aunts, my father and then, to an extent, by a combination of myself, Putul and Annie—and yet I was looking for an anchor, a place where I could be me and live the way I liked. Now, finally, in my own home, I hoped to heal my soul on my own terms.

Initially, I did not value the experience and skills I had gained while living in the spinal centre accommodation. But I realized slowly that I had probably undergone the worst and most difficult kind of training to manage by myself over there. Living in this two-bedroom flat was, in comparison, like being in heaven—managing it was not going to be as difficult as I had imagined.

❦

Having lived a very basic existence since my accident, just surviving each day for years, suddenly the luxury of having a home and the freedom to do as I wished had its own effect on me. I went a little berserk for the next two years, treating myself royally and enjoying life to the utmost. And my partner in crime turned out to be Vikas. It was a crazy time, when we would have common friends over nearly every day, go to a pub every week and, at times, go for long drives out of Delhi. We were even chastised by a cop for drinking next to a liquor shop! It was as though we bore each other company for the craziest of things.

It wasn't long after the Nainital trip that Vikas and I became very close friends. There was no reason for us to be such good friends, with him being seven years younger than me—a generation gap by many standards. But we really enjoyed being together. It was perhaps our differences that we appreciated the most. Why Vikas enjoyed being with me I do not know, but one of the main reasons why I liked being with him was because he was the only person I knew who did not consider me disabled and actually tried to get to know the person I was within my physically imperfect body. Everyone I knew apart from him had their affection, concern, liking or any other feeling towards me tainted to some extent by my disability. Vikas was the only person who expected something from me—he expected his friendship returned in equal measure.

There is a very thin line between friendship and love. Without even realizing how it happened, one regular evening in December 1999, we simply expressed our love to each other, which had previously been unknown even to ourselves. It was the most unexpected turn of events. Vikas was just killing time at my place, chatting with me, because he was an hour early for a blind date that he had set up. And then, out of the blue, without any warning, we kissed. It was the most outlandish behaviour for both of us! Neither of us had consciously thought that anything like this could ever happen.

Vikas was so much younger than me, pulsating with energy and youth and very popular with the girls we knew. And, aware as I was of my shortcomings, I was sure that he could have never been attracted to me physically. I was no Andrew who could have his Nina hug him and kiss him as he proposed marriage to her. I was a disabled woman who couldn't have any man interested in her romantically. I had accepted that such a thing was just not possible.

And yet, we kissed…the most perfect kiss. It was after several minutes that we came to our senses and parted awkwardly, apologizing to the other.

Even today, I don't know what pushed us that day. It was all very strange. Totally confused by my own actions, I said, 'Vikas, just forget about what happened. I am not the kind of person who can handle short-term relationships.'

Sounding a little embarrassed himself, he responded: 'Well, neither am I.'

Neither of us quite knew what was happening. Vikas very hurriedly left soon after, ditching his blind date and going home directly. I was left alone, trying to make sense of what had happened and the implications it might have. But, just for a moment, I was willing to accept that it was it was the most beautiful and natural thing to have happened. I had butterflies in my stomach.

On reflection, though, the incident caused a numbness in my mind. I had no idea what I was supposed to think about it. Was it a good thing to happen, or was it wrong? I didn't know. I was scared about how I would face Vikas the next day in the hospital. Was he going to be angry with me, or think of me as someone with questionable character? I did not want to lose him as my friend because of an accidental kiss. I spent a sleepless night, feeling anxious about what was going to come next. I am sure Vikas too must have grappled with his own confusion that night.

The next day, I met Vikas at the lunch table at the centre. He behaved as though nothing had happened. That suited me just fine. I played along and, within moments, everything was back to normal. As it happened, however, that kiss marked the start of a long and intimate relationship between us.

To say that we knew of our love for each other at the time would probably be wrong. We were very fond of each other and liked being together. Whether we had a future together was too difficult to think about and therefore never discussed. And so we kept up a façade of being good friends for everybody. Nobody knew of our relationship because disclosing it at a time when everything was so unclear even to us would have meant endless questions and doubts brought forth by everybody, including our family and friends. It was easier to just let it remain between us. As time passed, of course, we fell deeply in love. But our love remained a secret the two of us shared for years, learning not to put it into words even to each other.

It wasn't easy for me to maintain this two-faced approach towards our relationship. As any girl would, I too wanted to scream to the world and tell everybody how attractive I was to someone. Any girl would feel the way I was feeling, but my enthusiasm was probably much more magnified as I had previously convinced myself that this was an impossible thing. I wanted desperately to be able to share my joy in this newfound affection with at least somebody. Alongside, it wasn't easy to love someone so deeply and not expect anything in return. It required tremendous courage to love unconditionally and to accept whatever came my way. I always overdid things to prove my affection. I wanted to ensure that I did not fall short in pleasing Vikas, to the extent that I started pampering him. I was tormented with self-doubt and thought that I was not good enough for him. It was a constant fear that he would leave me and move on to someone better soon. It was only over time that I learnt to enjoy love as long as it lasted. I had no idea how long that would be, but I eventually stopped torturing myself because I wanted to enjoy every moment of it. Over the years, we developed a very mature and self-contained relationship that was free of doubt and never discussed with anybody else.

The most important thing I learnt from Vikas during that time was to accept people as they were and to appreciate whatever they did. This was something he taught me by simply accepting me just as I was and appreciating me at times when I didn't manage things too well. This helped me to start

accepting Meera as an important part of my life when it came
to my relationship with Daddy. I could now understand how
important companionship was—especially for Daddy, who just
wasn't the kind of person who could lead a life alone. I could
see that it wasn't for me to feel anger about their relationship—
the two of them had their own journey together, just as I had
mine with Vikas. And I could appreciate Meera for standing
by Daddy during good as well as bad times. The happiness
of having Vikas in my life erased the bitterness I had allowed
to fester in my mind against Daddy and Meera for all these
years. It was because of Vikas that I was able to accept their
togetherness and free myself of the pain I had inflicted on
myself because of my resentment. I felt not only lighter and
stronger but also much closer to Daddy.

⚘

Vikas and I were very different. He spent his life in fast motion,
as though trying to get more than twenty-four hours' worth
from every day. He not only spoke very fast but also wanted
fast results, fast responses, fast action, fast everything. I never
heard him say he was getting bored as he always had so much
to do. He was always energetic, never seeming to tire, with his
mind sharply active even long after midnight. I, on the other,
had lived life in slow motion, accepting delays easily and with
little on my agenda for days that included nothing other than
following a routine I was always bored of. I liked to sleep early,
and I tired quickly because of my disability too. I needed a lot
of bracing up to match Vikas's speed and passion for life.

Vikas loved to socialize with many people, while I enjoyed
being with only close friends—probably because I knew the

taste of rejection and was aware that most friends around us were there for only good times and fun. Despite this, because of Vikas, I learnt to be more social and enjoy being with people. He decided to introduce me to all the friends with whom he spent time after work. I was excited about meeting them; but, at the same time, I was nervous and self-conscious because I was worried about their reaction when they saw me, a disabled lady so much older than them. But I must say that I did not *feel* older than Vikas—being with him allowed me to experience the life that I had missed out on when I was his age because of my accident.

What gave me strength to go out and face the possible rejection was Vikas backing me despite his own uncertainty about how his friends would react towards me. I was his friend, and he expected all his friends to accept me if they considered him their friend. All those who couldn't accept me were to no longer be his friends either. He had no qualms about giving up such friends as in his mind it was crystal-clear that people who discriminated against me because of my disability were not worthy of being his friends. He proved his friendship to me thus, and it was I who felt compelled to prove myself worthy of his friendship. And it was his strong belief and unwavering faith in me that made me actually believe in my own worth as a person.

Vikas and I were always to be found together. All his friends knew this, and it wasn't long before they became my friends too and spent a lot of time at my place. One of his closest friends was Manoj. They had met at a common friend's house but had now become close and often met without the common friend along. Manoj had recently finished his studies to become a software engineer and taken his first job. Vikas and Manoj were like brothers who stood by each other regardless of whether they agreed or disagreed about things. There was a lot of affection between them. And because of his non-judgemental nature, Manoj became a very good friend of mine as well. The three of us usually spent all our evenings together.

Another friend was Sachin, with whom we would start AccessAbility much later. Vikas knew Sachin through Manoj as the two of them studied together, and he became our friend too. Sachin joined us only occasionally, though. He was the cool, good-looking guy who had a knack for being good company. Anybody who knew him was very fond him.

Apart from Manoj and Sachin, there was a large group of friends who were ready to party any time. My house became the party place, and the round dining table stood witness to all the crazy times we had. Looking back, I can say that we had the wildest two years of our lives during that time. Anyone could host a get-together at my flat on the condition that both Vikas and I were invited. None of us was really professionally satisfied with what we were doing. While we continued working, it was more because the fact of working was a necessity. What was more important to all of us was our evenings together. I started to enjoy life rather than simply live out every day.

≻≍≺

The strangest thing was that somehow my disability no longer mattered to me. I seemed to have forgotten about it. Vikas expected me to lead a regular life, just like all his other friends, and wanted me to be a part of all the fun. He was sometimes ruthless in his expectations, asking things of me that were too difficult for me to achieve. But, then again, it was those very expectations that forced me to challenge myself and my capabilities. I would often fight with him for expecting me to be a part of everything and plead with him to leave me alone so that I could take a break and rest. Exhausted by the busy social schedule, I sometimes wanted him to go out alone with his other friends—but he was adamant that he would go only if I accompanied him.

I hated Vikas when he could not see how tired I was, or how swollen my feet were from sitting for too long. None of this mattered to him. But now, when I look back, I believe that it was his indifference towards my disability that dictated my future and made me challenge myself further and further, forcing me to cross my own boundaries again and again. I set out to prove myself worthy of his love and trust and, most importantly, satisfy his expectations of me.

For Vikas, everything was either black or white. He was able to judge people quickly and predict the future based on the present. I lived my life in greys, always worried about making the wrong decision, not sure of what would be right. For him, it had to be a yes or a no—he did not leave any space for maybe. Eventually, thanks to Vikas, I learnt to be surer of what I wanted; thanks to me, he learnt to let some matters pass.

The one thing that anyone acquainted with us knew was how much the two of us fought. We fought over anything and everything. Manoj started calling us 'Tom and Jerry' because it seemed that our fights were something we could not do without. Most evenings, a constant accompaniment to whatever plans we had together was our fights. Over time, Manoj was able to predict what we were going to fight about next and, before we could start, he would butt in and help cool matters off. Most often, the fights were childish and light-hearted. But probably one in every fifty fights was a serious one, when it felt as if it was the end for us. We would separate in a huff, with Manoj trying to pacify us. Invariably, though, in a couple of days—without either of us saying sorry, of course—Vikas and I would be back together, happily fighting away.

Vikas questioned everything and demanded change, while I adjusted to everything that came my way even if I was unhappy with it. He taught me to fight for my rights and not accept poor treatment just because I was disabled. Together, we worked towards fighting for the rights of disabled people everywhere.

Another major difference was that Vikas picked faults in people, while I hardly ever judged anyone. I was probably the one Vikas had the most problems with. He would drive me crazy by pointing out my shortcomings and telling me what to do and how to improve. He was my biggest critic, pushing me to better myself. I often had to remind him that he was a man and not expected to nag constantly, especially since I, as woman, never nagged him!

Vikas was a perfectionist, while I accepted mediocrity. It was the high bar set by him in the way we lived or worked that made me raise my own standards too. He could do anything, saying 'It can't be rocket science'. Staying cool in difficult situations was his specialty, while I was the most tense person ever, worrying about every small thing and nervous about trying new things. Vikas was a night person and would come alive in the evenings, while I was a day person who wanted the comfort of bed as soon as it was past eleven. And while Vikas loved to drink, I loved to eat. He loved sweets, while I loved savouries. In other words, Vikas was from Mars and I was from Venus.

And yet, even though we were so different, we were still attracted to each other and could not think about being apart.

Book 3

Learning to Fly

16

I could not at that time spot any patterns that were forming in my life. The wheels of time were turning and I was connecting to the world I had been exiled from for years, but I had no idea in what direction I was heading. Life never failed to surprise me. But one thing was for sure: I knew that I was strong enough to face anything. I was happy, and I was no longer alone. I had Vikas with me.

I got an invitation to participate in a fifteen-day training programme organized by the United Nations Economic and Social Commission for Asia and the Pacific (UN-ESCAP) in Bangkok, Thailand. I was to attend training by master trainers from all the ESCAP countries in 'Non-Handicapping Environments for the Disabled and the Elderly'. I had no idea what non-handicapping environment meant, but that didn't matter much. The only information that sounded important was that there was an all-expense paid training programme in Bangkok that I could go for.

The problem, however, was that I was in the hospital, recovering from a lung collapse, even though I was almost ready to be discharged. I didn't quite know how to feel when I got the news—whether to be happy that I might be going to Bangkok, or sad that my health might not allow me to go. The programme was scheduled to begin in a week's time, and it seemed impossible that I would be able to attend it. I knew that if I asked anyone in the family they would discourage me, considering the fact that I was still recovering. But I was sure that if I did not go then the memory of the missed opportunity would stay with me for a long time, like the taste of sour grapes.

During a therapy session, I told Vikas about the possibility and casually asked if he would like to go. His response was instantaneous: 'Yes, of course. Let's go together.'

Go together? Was that a possibility? How could I go to a strange country with him? Yes, he was the person I was attracted to and was in a relationship with—but how could I burden him with assisting me on the trip? He would abandon me, I thought, as soon as he realized exactly how much assistance I needed in my activities of daily living. My mind raced with such fears until I looked into his eyes. His gaze gave me more assurance than any words could have and filled me with a sense of trust.

'But what about my lung collapse?' I said to him.

He very coolly replied, 'You have a paramedic going with you—why are you worried?'

Vikas's confidence and practical assessment of the situation put me at ease. I agreed, exclaiming: 'Okay, let's go!'

Having Vikas by my side, I understood, was giving me the courage to take chances in life instead of constantly playing safe. This was a big step for me because just a year ago, when I had gone to Nainital with my colleagues, I had realized that there were limits to what I could expect from others. But I had also by now learnt the difference between good-time friends and real friends. Vikas was my real friend—I knew that he would take care of me and not abandon me in a strange country. Through his behaviour with me, he was making me break free of the limitations I had set on myself because of one bad experience. He was helping me let go of a little bit of the negativity within me, me making me feel happier and lighter.

Everything moved very fast once we had decided. I told my family selectively about the trip, choosing not to reveal too many details to people I knew were not going to be comfortable with me travelling so far right after my illness. This included Daddy and Jiya; I knew they would be too worried to be able to wholeheartedly support my decision. Vikas left work early that same day and drove through Delhi traffic to get our recommendation papers signed by a government official—it was the last day to send our information to the training organizers. By evening, within a few hours of having thought of the plan, we were officially going! I was discharged the next day and we worked on getting our visas and tickets as quickly as possible. We took two weeks off from work and, on the fifth day after hearing the news, we were off to Bangkok.

Vikas had told his parents that he was going for training to Bangkok; they were very happy for their son and came to see him off at the airport. He had deliberately refrained from telling them that I was accompanying him because they didn't approve of me, and he didn't want to hurt them. The way in which Vikas's parents got to know of me was a very unfortunate one, and probably one of the most important reasons for them to dislike me without even knowing me. Vikas and I had had a witness to our first kiss—Putul, my carer. Suddenly, she started behaving very nastily and tried to blackmail me, saying that she would tell our parents about our affair. She did call our parents. But while Daddy very rightly told her to keep out of my personal life, Vikas's parents asked him to stay away from me because they saw no future for our relationship—mostly because of my disability. In their eyes, our relationship was doomed even before it had started. I therefore went to the airport alone, making sure that I didn't cross paths with Vikas's parents.

⚘

The fifteen days that we spent in Bangkok were invigorating, to say the least. It was the first time that I realized what the phrase 'time out of time' means. The world was in its place, keeping its tryst with night and day, hours of work and rest. Yet, exhilarated at being together in a new place, unshackled from the rigours of routine and convention, Vikas and I felt as if we were on a timeless plane. Anything and everything was an experience to be relished in each other's company.

The training programme was far beyond anything we had expected. They kept us busy with lectures, group work, fieldwork, etc., for ten to twelve hours a day. It was very intensive and regimented—a little like being in a military camp. The only time available to really relax and enjoy Bangkok was in the evenings. Everybody was tired from working so hard, but the two of us couldn't help ourselves—we absolutely had to go out and see the city every day. We couldn't possibly have returned without really experiencing Bangkok! What was good was that there was abundant fieldwork, so we saw some bits of the city in that way too.

Having said how busy they kept us, I must also state that it was a brilliantly organized and coordinated training programme. Each day kept all the participants alert and engrossed in the proceedings. As the term non-handicapping environment started making more sense to me, I grew awed by it. Vikas too was impressed by what the workshop had to teach us. It was an eye-opener for both of us. It made us realize the extent of benefits that non-handicapping and accessible environments could have on the lives of disabled people. Till now, we had known that elements like a ramp, an elevator a large restroom were important for a person using a wheelchair. But it was only there that we understood the complete picture, wherein a non-handicapping environment addressed needs of all kinds of disabilities. It was there that we truly understood the importance of accessibility for inclusion of a disabled person in society.

As we learnt more and more, I began to relate this concept with my earlier trip to the UK, when I had seen so many disabled people out and about on their own. It was possible for them to do so only because their environment was designed to be accessible to all users. It was that—an accessible environment without barriers—which enabled them to participate more fully in society and have more opportunities. I also started to appreciate that a non-handicapping environment was a most basic right for a disabled person—the right to be able to access all places with the same ease and dignity as a non-disabled person.

It was after understanding the importance of access that I could analyse the horrible experience of visiting the Kanyakumari temple in a different light. A couple of years ago, I had visited the temple with colleagues from the centre. I wasn't allowed to enter the temple in my wheelchair as it was considered impure. After a great deal of hesitation, I allowed one of my colleagues to carry me in his arms to have darshan of Goddess Kanyakumari. I didn't know better, so I agreed to be carried; but it was one of the most humiliating and embarrassing experiences of my life. Everybody ogled at us as my colleague carried me. Another colleague walked along with us, assuring each person who stared that I couldn't walk. It was quite a long way till the deity, and the only thing I was glad about was that I wasn't too heavy during those days and that the pandits were 'considerate' enough to not make us wait in the queue to get in.

Now, after this training, I could finally appreciate how justified was my anger at the humiliation I had been made to face—simply because of inaccessibility and the insensitive policy that did not allow me in my wheelchair. Anger was something that I had never really felt before when faced with discrimination. I had been humiliated, made to feel sorry for myself and torn to pieces countless times when, because of inaccessibility, I was either excluded from things or I had to take help from someone—but I had never outwardly expressed my anger over this till now. With the knowledge of non-handicapping environments and better understanding of my rights came anger with the system: why could it not provide a simple thing such as an accessible environment to me so that, as a disabled person, my life could be easier?

⁕⋇⋇⋇

Both Vikas and I had similar professional backgrounds—we were working in the field of rehabilitation of disabled persons. I do believe that it was because of this that the training had a similar impact on both of us. Until now, our understanding of disability had been limited to rehabilitation, and the hospital centre, where it was generally about fixing the problem with little practical concern about how the disabled person was going to manage in the real world, when they were out of the protected environment of the rehabilitation centre and back in their homes. It was in Bangkok that we recognized that rehabilitation at the hospital was just the tip of the iceberg. Far more important was actually integrating disabled people into society, and making society and environments accessible to them.

This exposure to the concept of non-handicapping environments made us both realize the gaps in the mainstreaming of disabled people. The more we discussed the issue, the more convinced we became about it. For sure, people with disabilities were excluded from education, employment or even a regular social life, and the biggest culprit in this was inaccessible environments. We realized just how India needed to work towards creating accessible environments across the country.

Vikas and I felt empowered by this new understanding of disability, accessibility and disability rights. The impairment of a disabled person was not the reason for his or her exclusion from society; in fact, it was society that posed handicaps in environments, which restrained disabled people from participating in them to the fullest degree. It was sheer good luck for me that both of us received this learning together and were shaken to the core owing to what we had learnt. It gave us both an interest in accessible environments and pointed us in the direction of our future. I am convinced that had only one of us got this opportunity to learn the future course of our lives would have been different. In fact, having my best friend share my field of interest as his own made working more fun for me, and vice versa. Over time, working for accessible environments became *our* passion.

As we returned to real life at the spinal centre, there was suddenly a great deal of impatience. We were bursting with enthusiasm about really contributing something of value—we wanted, at the very least, to share with others what we had learnt and experienced at the training. What made our urge stronger was our togetherness. We were like comrades marching towards a common goal, sharing our knowledge and discussing our future course. It was our togetherness in our passion for accessibility for disabled people that took us to greater heights—of further learning, further challenges and further achievements. Looking at it from a different perspective, it was also possibly our passion for the same cause that kept us together. Together we started looking in the same direction.

We were so excited that we actually connected with some likeminded friends and formed a non-government organization called Access to do meaningful work in the field. Considering that we were among the very few people in India who had undertaken this training till then and wanted to explore further, it wasn't long before we got our first project. It was to coordinate the first-ever awareness-raising project on the subject in India. The project, called 'Access for All', was funded by the government. A series of five training workshops was organized for participants from the entire country. I was the course coordinator for these workshops, with Vikas being one of the main presenters in the team.

What always amazed me was that even though Vikas was far sharper in his work compared to me, and we were equally trained, I was the main coordinator for this workshop and always recognized to a greater extent for the work we did together. But this never seemed to threaten Vikas's ego. We were a team, and he was my strongest supporter. It was as if he found satisfaction and a sense of achievement in ensuring that I was known, recognized and accepted by society.

For the workshops, the two of us authored a technical book called *Planning a Barrier Free Environment*. We had precisely a week to get it together as it was to go into printing before the trainings started. Though the book was only meant to be used for training purposes, for the next decade it was used as a technical guide for architects and civil engineers from across the country for getting specifications for building barrier-free buildings. Later, the book was nicknamed 'The Green Book' as its cover was green in colour. We had unknowingly made our first big contribution to the creation of barrier-free environments in India.

We were thrilled with this success, but Vikas was unable to share his joy over either co-authoring the book or doing such pioneering work with his parents because it was all with me. Somewhere deep down, I knew the loss he felt, even though we never talked about it. It was an unspoken understanding the two of us had: I knew how bad he felt about not sharing these things with his parents and that he was fighting turmoil within, but I also knew that I would be interfering if I spoke to him about it. His pain affected me just as much and I could not bring myself to fully share my joy and pride in the project with my family either.

✻❈✻

Following the book and the workshops, we conducted a number of government-funded 'access audits' of government buildings. An access audit is conducted primarily to identify the barriers in an environment and recommend solutions that can be retrofitted to make the environment more accessible to disabled people. While undertaking an audit is the first step towards making a infrastructure accessible, the sad part, we realized soon enough, was that very few of the audit reports were taken seriously by the building owners and only a handful actually got implemented on the ground.

I have no hesitation in saying that we were, in many ways, the pioneers in starting work on improving infrastructural accessibility for persons with disabilities in our country. We continued to get some work for the NGO; if nothing else, we'd get ourselves invited for lectures at architecture schools. Working for Access was deeply satisfying, even though there was hardly any money. It was not easy to find time to do what we really wanted to do aside from our full-time jobs, but we did.

It did not take us long to figure out that accessibility could not be truly improved by merely conducting access audits of places. There were some changes these audits made here and there, but nothing concrete. The whole process required a much better planned and a more holistic approach to be taken by the government. Accessibility and inclusion of disabled people had to be looked at with the same seriousness as any other developmental issue, and it was essential to integrate it with all developmental plans and programmes so that there were earmarked budgets to ensure accessibility. The importance of accessibility had to be recognized at the beginning of planning or at the design board stage. Real improvement could never be achieved with the government and builders thinking of at it as an add-on or afterthought. Just providing ramps and labelling spaces as 'accessible' did not foster inclusion. There was so much more to the subject that we didn't yet know and needed to learn.

We realized that we needed to study further to really do justice to the subject. The fifteen-day training we had attended was not adequate for us to label ourselves experts or access consultants and advising the entire nation on the subject. We knew that by continuing to work with accessibility with our half-baked knowledge we would probably be doing more harm than good for the country—and we definitely didn't want that. Not doing anything would be better than doing things in an unplanned manner, we decided. And hence Access was put on hold.

17

Though Access was not a full-time option for either of us at that time, it was more so for Vikas. He was just starting out in life and financial stability was crucial for him. Access, in our understanding, was not a financially viable full-time option. The salary that the spinal centre gave Vikas was not adequate either; so the best option, he decided, was to find a job as an occupational therapist in the UK, which was open for immigration, and settle there.

It was during this time, in November 2001, that the spinal centre sent Vikas to Italy and the UK for training in occupational therapy; he was even more convinced after this trip that he needed to move ahead. I introduced him to my first cousin Shipra, who was settled in the UK. Ajay, her husband, was a senior occupational therapist who had been working in the UK for several years. Vikas stayed a night with them in London before returning from his training and discussed the matter of working in the UK at great length with Ajay.

While Vikas was busy trying to make up his mind about moving to the UK, I finally got an allotment for my own flat close to the centre in February 2002. This was a plot that Daddy and I had fought hard for; it was an out-of-term allotment of a DDA flat on the basis of my disability—on grounds that

I needed a house walking distance from my office as it was difficult for me to travel.

It took years to get the allotment. To make my case heard in a government office was like screaming on an empty football field. When the officers turned a blind eye towards us, Daddy and I went to meet the Lieutenant Governor of Delhi, who headed the department. We met the LG twice; in spite of his approval for my case, the officers would not take heed. One officer very openly asked Daddy to pay him one lakh rupees to get the work done. Bribery was not something that went down well with us, and Daddy refused the proposition. As a result, my case was further delayed.

We went to meet the Minister of Urban Affairs next. He too approved my case and demanded immediate allotment. But the immediate action order by the Cabinet minister took nearly two years to finally get implemented. And when I did get my flat, the cost of it was twice as much as when we had made the application. If only we had paid the bribe, we could have saved ourselves a large amount of money by getting an allotment earlier, when the costs were lower! Once it was all over, I could not decide whether we had been right in not paying the bribe or simply impractical and foolish. Whatever it was, it had a heavy cost.

In any event, I finally got my house. Daddy, very patiently and with a lot of care, had the raw structure renovated and made accessible so that I could live there comfortably, with as much independence as possible. I moved into the house in March 2002.

Soon after moving into the new house, I got Ubbu, a little black pup. A pet dog was not something I had planned for myself. But it seems that dogs have a way of finding their masters and reaching them from faraway places. Ubbu was supposed to be Vikas's dog, coming to him after being passed on by several prospective owners. However, given that everybody in Vikas's house was working, it wasn't long before Vikas realized that he could not keep her. So, finally, it was my turn to inherit her.

Ubbu was a few weeks old when Vikas gave her to me. A mixed-breed puppy, she came to me with a couple of toys, made out of old socks, which she loved to nibble on. Being a dog lover, I loved her like my own child from the moment she came to me. Everything now started to revolve around her—keeping her entertained, her food, her toilet training, and so on. It took me nearly a month to give her a name. After careful thought, I decided to call her Ubbu. I wanted her name to be as unique as she was.

One of the friskiest dogs I have ever seen, she was a handful to manage. Every vet she went to through her life had the same comment to make about her: that they had never seen a dog as naughty as her. She would carefully smell each packet of bones on display for sale at the vet shop and select the one she wanted to be purchased for her. She was very special and very intelligent. Most of the time, it seemed to me that she understood each word we spoke and responded accordingly. She hated being referred to as a dog—in her dictionary, 'dogs' were strays, with whom she could not identify. She loved running out of the house and having us chase her to get her back inside. She was fussy about food and refused to drink milk even as a little pup. We tried feeding her everything vegetarian, from vegetables and fruits to dal—but she would stay hungry for days and not eat unless she was given chicken. In many ways, Vikas and Ubbu were alike: they were both very stubborn and loved being cosseted by me.

I was keen that Ubbu should love me the most and consider me her master. But the sad thing was that I could never play with her enough because of my poor mobility. As she grew older, she learnt to love me even though I was not the one to cuddle and pat her for very long; she understood my disability—and, because of that, my limitations. There was no doubt she looked to me as her master—or, as I like to refer to it, her mother. Over time, the two of us developed a very special relationship. She was a caring companion and gave me a lot of emotional support at various junctures in my life.

While on the one hand there was the happiness of having my own house and Ubbu, on the other hand was anxiety and nervousness about Vikas shifting soon to the UK. He had already acquired all the information regarding getting a job in the UK and needed to take an exam to get certified for working in the UK. The only centre to write the exam was in the UK. Things started working out for him quickly. He got an exam date and Ajay and Shipra offered him their hospitality in London. Staying with them was the best option as he would also be able to get last-minute tips from Ajay thanks to his tremendous experience. There was nothing left for Vikas to do now, except to get a flight ticket and study. His shifting to the UK was quickly going from a possibility to a reality.

While I was working to arrange his stay in London with my cousin, Vikas was making strange plans. He had decided that I was going to accompany him on the trip. I don't know from where he got the idea that I was going to go with him. In my mind, going with him was out of the question—it wasn't like going on a road trip to Shimla. In any case, why should I go? It wasn't my examination! Besides, I didn't have enough money to take a holiday in Europe, let alone pay an extra share for my carer, who didn't even have a passport. 'I can't go,' I said sternly, but Vikas persisted. He wasn't going to give up easily.

'Don't take your carer. I'll help you,' he insisted. 'Come on, you can arrange money enough for yourself,' he continued. 'Chalo na, please?'

I don't know why I could never refuse him. Why was I so helpless in front of him? Yes, Vikas was very insistent and a true stubborn Taurus; but I too had always been a fiercely strong-minded person. However, when it came to him, he could make me do anything. It wasn't as if he was making me dance to his tune; it was probably more about me not wanting to hurt him. He made me take reckless decisions quite easily. Reckless was how my life could be defined in any case—I was spending it with a man who I knew was going to leave very soon. And yet, I wanted to do as he asked.

For Vikas, with me along, just going to London was not enough. He wanted us to travel to other parts of Europe since we were already there and the major expense of air travel had already been paid. He made me do extensive web research on the options open to us. After lengthy discussions, arguments and a lot of research, we zeroed in on Paris and Brussels as these places just about fit into our budget. Vikas knew how to derive the maximum out of anything—whether it was from me, the trip or our budget.

The dates of the trip were decided based on Vikas's exam date. They happened to coincide perfectly with a fifteen-day volunteering experience we were invited to by Pauline Hephaistos Survey Projects to help with the survey for the *London Access Guide*, a travel guide for disabled people visiting London. Post the survey, we were going to travel in Europe for a week. Everything was working out well: after the one-day exam, we had at hand a two-month holiday in Europe.

We made all our bookings from Delhi itself. We got our tickets and visas organized and were all set to leave within a month. Ubbu, who was now three months old, was going to stay with Daddy, who always had his door open for her whenever I travelled. He never complained about having to keep her, even though she was very naughty and not easy to manage. Daddy had by now moved back to Faridabad to live with my grandmother, who was finding it difficult to continue living alone because of her age.

18

We landed in London on a bright afternoon in May 2002. This, without a doubt, was the best time of the year to visit London since the weather was excellent. I had mixed feelings about the trip. I was excited about our holiday, but at the same time I was very nervous about being dependent for such a long time on someone other than my carer. Vikas, on the other hand, was very happy to be making this trip with his best friend, the person he loved dearly, and nothing else made any difference to him.

I do not know where our friendship ended and love began, but having my best friend as my lover had its own benefits. Each time we fought as lovers, the friendship held us together; and when we fought as friends, love kept us close—we were, thus, inseparable. As always, throughout the trip, we had many arguments. But love and friendship combined together to make it a thoroughly pleasurable trip.

As we walked out of Heathrow, we spotted Shipra and Ajay waving at us from a distance. It was a long drive to their house in Epping. They lived in a duplex, with the sitting-cum-dining area, the kitchen and a bathroom on the ground floor, and the bedrooms on the first floor. They had arranged for a folding cot for me, and it was set up on the ground floor. I was going to be occupying their sitting room as my bedroom for two months, but they didn't seem to mind at all. Both of them were very warm and welcoming and made sure we had a good time while we were with them. Shipra, who was ensuring my comfort in every way, reminded me of Jiya. It was enough that they took us in, but their kindness and generosity made them make us a part of their lives.

Vikas's exam was in a week. He used all his time till then to pick Ajay's brain to understand the system of work of occupational therapists in the UK. Vikas knew that the test would relate more to the practical aspects of working in UK than to theories of occupational therapy. When the day arrived, Vikas left home early and travelled to Cambridge to write his exam. He returned early evening with the usual smile on his face. He was satisfied with his exam and was happy with the discussions he had had with Ajay all of the past week—that was exactly what was asked in the exam.

The most important task for which we had travelled was over—the rest was going to be all fun!

We joined the group for the *London Access Guide*; there were about eighteen people who had got together for the access survey. The group comprised young Brits who were in some way connected to the Christian group attached to the St Paul's School. The group was to assemble and stay at the youth hostel in London. It was a novel experience to live with native young Brits and get a glimpse of their lifestyle and culture.

There were three other disabled people in the group. One of the aims of the project was also that non-disabled people in the group have an opportunity to work and stay with disabled persons and be able to assist them. The idea of non-disabled people living with disabled people and assisting them in their daily living activities—to foster awareness and inclusion of disabled people—was an extraordinary idea in itself. I could not imagine youngsters in India taking on such a responsibility even for a day, so I had to compliment the Brits for their community spirit. Being together like this helped in breaking barriers and increased sensitivity for everyone in the group. The project provided a unique opportunity for learning and sharing about disability.

For the actual survey, we were divided into groups of four, with one group leader and one disabled person per group. Every morning after breakfast, there was a group meeting wherein sites for survey were given to the group, along with packed lunches that always comprised a sandwich, a small packet of crisps, a nutri-bar and a juice tetra-pack. After the morning briefing, all the teams would set out for their tasks. Using the London tube, we would go to our designated areas, which were invariably places of tourist interest since the access guide was meant for tourists. For us, who were really tourists in London, this was ideal. We had an opportunity to see London for free in a way that no tourist would get to do even if they paid a fortune for it. In fact, even our stay and food was taken care of by the group.

Vikas and I were really impressed by the project. Having an access guide for all tourist areas in a city was such a useful concept, we thought, something that would have been very helpful if we had one for Delhi. There were so many instances when we wanted to go out but just did not know which places were going to be accessible for a wheelchair user like me. In the absence of that information, we were forced to frequent only a couple of tried-and-tested places. India had so many travel guides available in the market, but not one had any information on accessibility for the benefit of disabled travellers. It would be a small endeavour but with such great benefits—I suppose the people in charge, unfortunately, never saw a profitable business proposition in it. Or, perhaps, they had simply never thought about it at all.

We carried a dream with us from the UK—to be able to create such guides for travellers in India. We accomplished a part of that dream nearly eight years later, when we developed a travel portal with access information for places of interest in Delhi. We called the portal 'Free to Wheel'. The satisfaction we felt after accomplishing this was incomparable for both of us. We wanted to expand this to other Indian cities too, but as it would turn out, destiny had other plans.

❦

The last phase of our adventurous trip was a journey to Paris and Brussels. We knew we needed to scrounge during the Europe trip to get the maximum out of it. In Brussels, we had found an accessible youth hostel; but we were not sure where we could stay in France. The gentleman in charge of the *London Access Guide* had also published an *Access in Paris* guide; he recommended that we try an Etap Hotel—they were supposed to be a new chain of budget hotels with accessibility incorporated.

The day arrived for us to leave from the UK. We packed our stuff into two backpacks and picked up my sliding board, a device that I used to transfer in and out of a car or the bed. I held the sliding board in my lap, while one of the backpacks hung from my wheelchair back and the other from Vikas's shoulders. Vikas pushed my wheelchair throughout the trip— he was very energetic, never seeming to get tired after walking long distances along with me (even on the bumpy cobblestone roads of Old Brussels).

We reached Paris early in the afternoon. We were going to be there for just two nights; therefore, to make the most of our time, we decided to go straight to the Eiffel Tower, all our luggage hanging from our backs. We tried to enquire if the Paris metro was accessible, but people spoke only in French and it was difficult to communicate or get any information. We finally saw a symbol for accessibility next to the metro sign and assumed it must be accessible; even if it wasn't, it would probably be much better than the inaccessibility we faced in India. We purchased two metro tickets till the Eiffel Tower.

We were feeling very clever about saving money and time, but when we reached the platform we realized there were three huge steps to get on to the train. Vikas managed to get me up these without difficulty as he was used to carrying me up a couple of steps since most places we went out to in India were inaccessible. We got off at the station for the Eiffel Tower. The station turned out to be in the basement, one level down from the street. We looked for a lift or a ramp to get till the ground level but, to our horror, there was none. Trying to enquire was futile because of the language problem. We were stuck! We could neither return to Gare du Nord from this station, nor could we get out of the station, as there was a flight of about fourteen steps.

I was getting worked up. I was worried and panicky, with knots in my stomach, and nagged about what we were going to do now. Thankfully, Vikas kept calm and tried to calm me down too, knowing full well that he had no other option but to pull me up all these steps. Getting me up fourteen steps, with my wheelchair, was not a joke. He knew it was too far to pull me up alone. And yet, given that we had no options, he started. He managed fourteen steps without much visible difficulty; it was after that that he started tiring. I sat tight on my chair, trying to wheel myself backwards so I could give him some support, but I knew how useless that was. I was feeling rotten and cursing myself for coming on this trip. Wasn't this the reason people looked down on disabled people? It was ironic that these steps had been put in by the same society that considered being disabled the same as being helpless. This was so unfair to both of us—I didn't want to put my friend through this.

Vikas just kept at it. He slipped out of his shoes to get a better grip with his feet while pulling me up. I was petrified. My wheelchair could have easily slipped out of his hands at any moment, or he could have lost his balance and both of us would have gone rolling down and hurt ourselves severely, in this strange country where we couldn't even communicate. I am sure Vikas was aware of this too.

Other people at the station just watched us in awe, and not one person came forward to help. At least, even if facilities are not accessible in India, people would have come forward to help without even being asked. With all these thoughts running through our minds, we somehow made it safely to the top and just sat there to catch our breath, amazed at what we had just done.

We were always angered by inaccessibility and the poor design of spaces that so easily excluded people. It is not easy being a disabled traveller. One can never travel impromptu; one needs to have done a lot of homework on the accessibility of a place even before reaching it. Architects, designers and planners have often a distorted understanding of accessibility, because of which even spaces that are signposted as being accessible are often unusable by disabled people. Also, invariably, only the most expensive options are accessible—such as using taxis or staying in luxury five-star hotels—which is ridiculous, given that people with disabilities are not the richest members of society.

Vikas and I sat for a while, ranting our hearts out about inaccessibility. Somehow, criticizing others made me feel a lesser culprit for making it so difficult for Vikas. I couldn't help thinking at that moment that Vikas would probably have had a better time without me.

But Vikas was selfless in his love and friendship. I guess this was the reason why I could never refuse him anything. At that time, I took all of Vikas's caring and support for granted; but today, when I look back, I realize what an extraordinary person and a friend he was. Taking responsibility for taking care of me, or even just standing by me through everything, was not an easy task. It meant helping me in grooming and using the toilet, apart from pushing my wheelchair around and also facing discrimination along with me. No one I had ever known would do this for me apart from Daddy. But now I had Vikas too. My best friend.

In spite of the poor local travel experience, we were overjoyed to be at the Eiffel Tower. Being there together was all that mattered. We forgot all the problems we had just faced as we stood close to each other on top of the tower, enjoying the view of Paris. Who could have imagined that I was the same person for whom doctors had given up hope ten years ago, saying I would live the life of a 'vegetable'? Here I was, miles away from home, enjoying the breath-taking view of Paris with the person I loved most in the world!

The next day, we went to the Louvre. Like children, we

were happy to see the masterpieces that till now we had only read about. We spent about four hours at the museum and, of course, it was not enough. We spent the rest of the day loitering on busy Paris streets, absorbing the culture. It was wonderful to be there, amongst the chic French women with haughty little Chihuahua dogs in their bags, and people sitting at roadside cafés and enjoying their drinks. It was all out of the movies for me. We had baguette sandwiches and crepes from roadside carts for our meals, then stopped at a café. I ordered an espresso, thinking it would be the same sweet, milky coffee that was served at Indian weddings. When I got it, I was most disappointed. Vikas enjoyed his cappuccino, laughing at me and saying he thought I knew what I was ordering. I had to drink that horrible concoction since we were paying so much for it.

We had the loveliest time in Paris without seeing the night life of the city, without dining at an elite French restaurant or doing all the exotic things that we imagine people do in Paris. Just being there together was enough for us—anything over and above that was a bonus.

Our next stop was Brussels. We had expected it to be a very official city, with its offices and headquarters for the EU and so many organizations; but it appeared to be a small city, with all touristy sights within walkable distance. The biggest problem, though, were the cobblestone streets I mentioned earlier. My wheelchair was difficult to push for Vikas on those roads. But the youth hostel, luckily for us, was in the Old Brussels area, and that was where all the monuments of tourist interest were.

We spent our two days wandering through all of Old Brussels and enjoying the magnificent architecture and loitering in the busy town centre. Vikas purchased a small gold locket for me as a memory of our Euro trip together. It was the cheapest piece of jewellery in the shop, but for me it is the most precious piece I possess, and I always wear it around my neck.

We started on our journey back to the UK with a heavy heart because it was not only the end of our Euro vacation but also nearing the end of our stay abroad. But I was happy because we had had a fantastic trip. Without Vikas, I know, I would have never taken this trip or travelled to Paris or Brussels. I was thankful that I had listened to my heart and agreed to come for the trip. Sure, we had uncountable fights and arguments all throughout, but the care with which Vikas assisted me these two months made me feel very secure with him. I had not felt the same with anyone else, and this sense of security was to remain forever. I was, without doubt, blessed to have Vikas in my life.

Vikas's results came a few days after our return to London. He had cleared the licensing exam!

19

Ubbu, who had grown a little bigger in these two months, was ecstatic to see me. She came running and jumped onto my lap, where she struggled to keep balance. She wouldn't let anybody come close to me for a long time, as if announcing that I belonged to her. She had developed some brown streaks on her black coat. Since she was a mixed-breed puppy, I had no idea what she was going to grow up to look like, and so this was a surprise.

My life was shaping up so well—a man I loved, my own home and a pet-child. There seemed to be nothing more that I could desire. But this bliss was to be short-lived. Within the next two months, my life took a drastic turn.

It wasn't long after our return that the moment for which I had been preparing myself from the day our affair began arrived. Vikas and I had known that this would come up and we would have to part sooner or later. But I guess no amount of preparation is ever adequate when it comes to parting with the person you love and who is also your only true friend. After being together for three years, it was as if I didn't know a life without Vikas. We had been doing everything together; now, to part so abruptly, for no fault, made me feel angry and helpless. I knew that if I were not disabled we could have married and been together, but the society we were a part of was not mature enough to accept us together. It seemed like a worthless reason for parting.

But I had known that this was bound to happen, that Vikas was meant to move on. Still, I would have done anything to avert it. However, I found some solace in the fact that he was moving on for better career prospects and not for another girl; my doubts about myself, my ability to be loved, were curbed. I was not losing him because of my shortcomings compared to someone else.

Since I had, deep down, been preparing myself for this moment, I was composed on the outside. But within I was breaking. I wanted to scream my lungs out, to vent my pent-up anger against society. How was I supposed to bid farewell to Vikas without a trace of sorrow? But this had been our pact, and this was the real test of love and friendship. I trained myself to appear calm by focusing on feeling happy for my best friend rather than mourning the loss of my love.

Vikas had worked hard to get this opportunity and was definitely looking forward to it. He too, like me, had been preparing for this day. At this stage in his life, the most important thing was his career. Going to the UK was the best option for him and I understood that well. I knew he had to go. No matter what, we knew we had no future together. So this was it.

Now more than ever, it was important for me to concentrate on my future and myself. I didn't want to be someone who would waste time wallowing in self-pity, especially because what was happening was through no fault of mine. With Vikas working towards improving his life, it was time for me to review my own professional status. It was immediately evident to me that I was not enjoying my work any longer. There was nothing new for me to learn at the centre, and there were no prospects for any sort of promotion. Somewhere inside me, I was becoming more interested in disability rights rather than accepting discrimination. Moreover, after the UN-ESCAP training, I had identified my area of interest, and it was very different from peer counselling.

I could have continued to work in barrier-free environments and taken Access further, but I needed to be better trained to do good quality work. I was terribly confused. I had no idea about what I should do—I had not really thought of myself as an independent professional for some time. The thought of Vikas leaving soon too added to my impatience and discomfort about my job. I did not want to continue being at the spinal centre without him—it would make me miss him even more.

I needed to get my act together quickly. I knew it was vital for me to get myself involved in doing something I enjoyed, something that made me grow at a professional level and gave me the opportunity to learn new things. The only thing, I realized, that could give me all this was further studies. When I look back, I wonder if I would have ever left my comfort zone of the non-demanding job at the spinal centre had it not been for Vikas's shift. This determination to study again, perhaps, was the silver lining to Vikas's move to the UK. I knew for certain that I had to find a new life for myself.

The thought of the emptiness and pain Vikas's departure was going to bring spurred me into action. I began to look at options more seriously. There was nobody I could discuss this with, not even Vikas or Daddy. Vikas was too busy preparing for his own new life and Daddy, as always, said 'Leave it to Sai Baba.' Neither of them was of any help to me at that point. I felt so directionless that I actually asked Daddy to have my horoscope read, hoping to get some answers from the stars.

One afternoon, I went with Daddy to a job fair organized by a new private university. The reason for going to that fair was not looking at educational options but meeting Daddy's friend, who was a professor at the university and also an astrologer of some eminence. He had asked us to come and meet him at the fair as he was on duty there for that day. He had already made astrological calculations based on my date and time of birth and was going to tell me something about my future. This, I hoped desperately, would point me to the direction in life I should take.

The fair was full of young students seeking information and getting admitted into various courses offered by the university. Daddy and I sat at the reception, waiting for the gentleman to arrive. To pass the time, I started browsing through the courses the university had to offer. The programme in architecture technology seemed interesting and I started enquiring about it. It was a full-time two-year diploma course in architecture technology. This university had an affiliation with Edexcel, a British company that was certifying this as a professional course.

I enquired about the minimum educational requirements, age limit for admission and other such criteria. As it turned out, much to my pleasant surprise, all that mattered to the university management was the enrolment of a large number of students. So any person, no matter what age, gender, physical capabilities, etc., who had completed their schooling, was eligible to apply. My disability and my age were not issues for them—unlike in regular architectural colleges in India, where both my age and disability disqualified me. It was too tempting to resist. Considering my interest in inclusive environments, this seemed to be just the thing for me to do.

I thought about it for a bit, not sure if I was hearing and understanding everything correctly. Then I expressed my interest to Daddy and, before I knew it, we were enquiring about the fee structure, the college address and timings. Soon, I was writing a test for scholarship, and I had an admission letter with a fifty per cent scholarship for the first semester in my hand! My session was going to begin by the second week of August.

Everything that happened that day was strange. All of a sudden, I was going to become a full-time student, at my age and with my severe disability. I had to be out of mind! After all, I had a job and a comfortable house—what more could I be asking for? I have no idea where I got the courage to take that impulsive decision—perhaps it was the combination of the misery about Vikas's leaving and Daddy's support. I could remember Mr Dutt asking me what was it that I wanted to do in the future six years ago; I had dismissed higher education on the grounds that it would be too difficult for me. But now, finally, it was time for me to act.

It was the most rash and least considered decision I had taken till then in my life. I left behind everything that day— all that was mine, everything that defined me—in pursuit of my passion for inclusiveness. I knew instinctively that it was the only thing that would keep me from falling apart after Vikas left—it was the only way for me to rise instead of fall. The astrologer friend of Daddy's we were there to consult was eventually unable to meet us, but I didn't need his services any longer. My future was decided for now.

That evening, I told Vikas about my plans. He didn't respond, thinking I was just fooling around. I repeated myself, making sure I had his full attention. He didn't know how to react for a while—he seemed completely taken aback. I couldn't tell how he felt about it, whether he thought I was being foolish or if he was glad. It was only much later, when I started attending college, that I knew he was happy for me. Each evening, he had lots to ask me about my day. Sometimes, I could sense a hint of pride in him, as if I had reaffirmed to him that he had made no mistake in loving me the way he did.

In the meanwhile, there were lots of things to deal with. I was going to leave my own home and shift to rented accommodation closer to college and become a full-time student after a gap of eleven years. Architecture required a lot of drafting and, with my paralysed hands, I was not sure if I could manage it. Moreover, I had no idea how this would benefit me in actual terms. I didn't know if I would get a job after completing the course, or if I would be able to make Access more lucrative. I was just following my passion.

I finally quit the spinal centre even before Vikas. I was glad about that, as I knew that being there without him for even a day was going to be dreadful. I moved to the rented accommodation in Faridabad before Vikas left India. I was happy about that too, as I knew that living alone in the house where Vikas and I had shared so much was going to be painful. I was, after all, building myself a brand new life.

20

My new life as a full-time student brought with it many changes and challenges. All of these were very welcome, since they were going to help me continue living life in the manner Vikas had taught me—happy, believing in myself and having the courage to take big steps.

Daddy supported me in my decision to pursue further education and to shift to a rented house closer to the university; but the rest of the family felt that I should not leave the spinal centre and, in any case, architecture would be a difficult course for me given my severe disability and paralysed hands. It was only Daddy who believed in me and encouraged me. Despite having worked so hard to make my new flat comfortable for me to live in, he, without question, helped me relocate only a few months later. My own flat, in turn, was given out on rent. We had returned from Europe in early June; by the end of August 2002 I had moved to Faridabad and started my new course. Just a fortnight before, I could not have imagined that my life was going to take such a drastic turn.

Daddy started living with me at the rented place in Faridabad. Since this house was close to my grandmother's, he was able to visit her often. I had been living separately for six years now, so it was lovely to have him around, taking care of me after all this time. This was the most enjoyable and meaningful time spent with Daddy that I remember today—it was the time when I bonded most with Daddy. Earlier, when I was living with him, my disability had weighed very heavy on both of us. But I was a much stronger person now, and Daddy too seemed far more settled. He was comfortable with himself and his retirement, and seemed more relaxed and happy. Meera, even nine years after Daddy's return from Nigeria, continued to be like a guest who came and left at her convenience. Since Daddy did not mind, I did not mind either. I had accepted her part in Daddy's life and actually started enjoying her presence whenever she was around.

I also got a new carer—Ritu, a young girl from the state of Chhattisgarh. Her father's income lay in farming, but with a number of siblings there wasn't much available for everyone. And so Ritu had come to Delhi to find work without the permission of her parents. But, of course, they were glad when she got a job and was safe and happy. Ritu was a hard worker. But, more importantly, she was a mature person who was able to live with Daddy's bickering without bringing it to my notice since it inevitably resulted in tension between me and him.

Ubbu and Ritu became good friends. Ubbu treated Ritu as one of her pals—she always wanted to play with her and constantly troubled her, trying to get her attention while she was busy with work. Ubbu was still very young and very naughty. In the mornings, while I would be getting ready for college, she would invariably run off with the undergarments that lay on my bed as I bathed. It was a time when all my underwear had little teeth holes courtesy of Ubbu. She was light on her feet and ran like the wind and could easily jump over high fences. Most of Ritu's time was consumed looking after the pup, chasing her as she ran out of the house. Ubbu ensured there wasn't a moment of rest in the house. At times, she would keep busy by pulling out my clothes from the cupboard and chewing on them, or jumping and scampering around the house, across the sofas and beds, dislodging all the pillows and cushions, or simply pulling out vegetable peels from the kitchen dustbin and spreading them around the house.

We engaged a dog trainer to train Ubbu, hoping that it would tame her high spirits a little. Every day, as soon as the trainer arrived, Ubbu would hide under the bed. She had to be pulled out to go out with him for her training session. She picked up all he had to teach quickly, but her problem was that she did the tricks only when she was alone with the trainer and never in front of us. Within two months, the trainer gave up, saying that it was beyond him to train Ubbu. Not even a raise in salary could make him stay. Ubbu, of course, was happy to have him gone. I gave up my hopes of training her as a service dog. She didn't need to do any tricks to get my love—she was my naughty little child, about whom the entire world had complaints.

Vikas left in mid-September 2002. Just before he left, his grandmother had a fall and was diagnosed with a spinal injury. The doctors gave little hope because she was frail and old. Vikas loved his grandmother very much and she had often lived with him since his childhood. It broke his heart to leave his grandmother in that condition. He believed he could do a lot to help improve her condition, but there was no way he could stay back. He was utterly torn. His concern, even moments before boarding his flight, was the wish that he could be with his grandmother during the time. She passed away the next day. Vikas started his life in the UK sad and alone.

One of the challenges that I faced in college was that I was almost twice as old as my classmates, and older than most of my lecturers too. It was quite awkward for me to be sharing the classroom with young eighteen-year-olds straight out of school. There was a vast generation gap. I didn't know what to talk to them about, and all of them felt awkward about spending time with a thirty-two-year-old disabled lady. I was old enough to be their aunt—and all of us were very conscious of this. Initially, most of the students were even scared of approaching me! But, in time, it all settled down and I found my place in my batch. Everybody became my friend and everybody liked me, especially as I wasn't part of any of their childish antics or intrigues.

It was during that time that I realized why I didn't really have any close friends except Vikas. I was never doing the same things people my age were doing, and my life never seemed to have any similarities with that of the people around me. There was no common ground to connect on. Women my age were living all around me, but I didn't know even one of them. While they bonded with each other over evening strolls around the colony—discussing children, in-laws and maids—I was sitting at my drawing board and getting my assignments ready.

In the early days at the college, while my batch mates were busy getting to know each other, making friends and forming groups they were going to hang out with, I didn't really fit in anywhere. But I wasn't worried about this. Rather, I was consumed by my own set of self-doubts. I was worried about what would happen if I was not be able to manage to complete the course, considering that any design course demands a lot of hand skills. I had nothing to fall back on as my house had already been rented out and I had quit my job. I couldn't go back anywhere. But Daddy encouraged me by constantly, saying that he believed in me and was sure I could do it. Taking his words to heart, I worked very hard and, to my surprise, turned out to be one of the best students in the class. I guess it was easier for me to remain focused on my work compared to my young classmates! Being one of the best in class was strange to me after living what I had always thought was a mediocre kind of life—but I liked it!

My faculty at the university was most accommodating. I often felt some of them were a little intimidated by me. After all, a number of them were younger than me. Initially, I found it strange addressing the younger faculty members as 'madam' or 'sir', like all the other students, but it wasn't long before I adjusted to my environment and was, in the classroom, as young as all my classmates. In spite of my intimidating aura, I was not excused from missing any of my assignments, whether it was working on the drawing board or making architectural models. I worked hard in class and at home and managed to do all my board assignments and, in time and with practice, became good at them. But making models was absolutely not possible for me with my hands. Therefore model-making became a family exercise, with my father and Ritu helping me out. So much new learning was invigorating, and it made me feel youthful and carefree.

The only places accessible to me in the whole university were my studio and the computer room. There was no other place I could go to—not even the restroom. As always, my biggest challenge was managing my incontinence. My bladder training and practice of remaining thirsty and not drinking any liquids for hours together helped me attend my classes. Despite this, there were accidents; on those bad days, I had to leave for home early and miss my classes. These accidents never failed to pull me down. I would often return home and cry helplessly for not being able to manage. On those days, consoling me, Daddy would say: 'Beta, what cannot be cured must be endured.' Those words he quoted made sense to me and gave me strength and acceptance.

My batch mates were either people who had not scored too well in their class twelve board exams or those who had not cleared the entrance exams for the courses of their choice. They were all from affluent families and had aspirations of going abroad for further studies. Their aspirations acted as a trigger for me to think in that direction too. If they could dream of going abroad for higher studies, then I surely could dream of going to the UK for the same purpose? This thought was like music to my ears. Very early in my course, I started considering the option of going to the UK to continue studying after I finished my diploma. I had no clarity regarding which course or how I would go, but I had two years to figure that out.

≈≈≈

Vikas had started a new life in UK; I had started one at college. Despite the distance and the new experiences, I am not sure if anything changed in our relationship. Yes, we were physically apart now, but in spirit we were still connected. Without communication with one another, the day seemed incomplete. Among the many tasks that both of us undertook in our lives, one of the most important ones was chatting with each other on the Internet every day. I can never forget the restlessness and emptiness of days when my Internet connection would be down, which was a common occurrence in Faridabad at that time.

As we chatted till very late hours, Ubbu would, without fail, scratch the back of my chair in an effort to call me to bed to sleep. Since she was still not fully grown, she used to sleep with me, and the two of us managed to fit in my single bed. I would cajole her like a child every day:'Beta, you sleep, I'm just coming.' She would be sprawled across my bed, fast asleep, by the time I reached it after I had finished talking to Vikas.

Everything about Ubbu—her naughtiness, her love and her caring—seemed to keep the emotional void of Vikas's moving away in check. She was entirely self-absorbed in her pranks, like any small child, and yet was very sensitive to my moods. Though Daddy was the one who toilet-trained her and kept her under control and Ritu was the one who took her for walks and fed her, Ubbu was devoted to me—like a child who is most attached to her mother irrespective of what anyone else does for her.

Vikas was employed as an occupational therapist at the Wexham Park Hospital in Slough, London. He was quick to adjust and learn the work culture of the hospital in his new country. It wasn't a surprise for any one of his friends in India when we got to know that he was well-liked by all his team members. Promotions at work came to him easily and quickly.

But while things were A-class at work, and his performance was remarkable, at a personal level, Vikas was not doing so well. He was terribly homesick. Even though he was quick at making friends, he missed all his Indian friends and the good times had in Delhi. He was staying in hospital accommodation, where he survived on ready-to-eat pizzas, noodles and macaroni and cheese as he preferred eating those things to having to cook. Had it not been for the satisfaction he got at work, he might have returned to India after just a few months. Vikas would visit India for a holiday twice a year. Every time he went back to the UK after his holiday, the first thing he did was to start planning for his next holiday—that was the only thing that helped him go on.

Aware of how much he missed us all and how alone he felt there, chatting with him over the Internet was the most important thing for me even on days when I was unwell. I wanted very much to be with him and share his pain. I had always teased Vikas for having never faced any adversity, and now the loneliness changed him. He lost his bubbly, excited nature and became more serious about everything, with a very high value placed on his family and friends. He seemed to mature into a strong man, taking care of everything.

I knew that Vikas missed me the most—there was no reason otherwise for him to spend his entire holidays with me—but we did not allow ourselves to discuss our love with each other, even if there wasn't a day that passed without our connecting. He would drive down daily to pick me up from my home, which was now more than twenty kilometres away from his house, and drop me back at night. We would mostly drive around those days, meeting up with friends at roadside parantha places or at pubs. We also made several trips to the mountains with friends, visiting Shimla, Manali and McLeodganj. Vikas loved driving and, with him, I had no problem in venturing anywhere. One occasion each year that Vikas made sure he was in India for was my birthday. Every year, he ensured that we celebrated it with many friends. He was always more excited about my birthday than me. While I would have been happy to just spend the day with him, Vikas ensured that he made it special. I don't remember celebrating any of Vikas's birthdays with such enthusiasm!

The only time I left the house except to go to college was when Vikas was in India. I didn't go anywhere or meet any friends otherwise. As with him in the UK, I had no social life without him. I remained busy with my studies, with Ubbu and Daddy and the daily chats with Vikas. I also cooked occasionally, along with Ritu.

Being apart, I realized, had not changed a thing in our relationship. In fact, we had started recognizing in greater depth the other person's importance in our lives and probably loved each other more than ever before. But we also knew that we had no future together as Vikas's parents would not accept me. At a certain level, there was a great deal of pain in our relationship, knowing that we could never be together; but we were able to rise above that pain and love selflessly, without being afraid of losing each other. We had an amazing relationship, wherein each of us was free to follow our own paths.

21

After settling down in his job, Vikas started exploring possibilities of enrolling for a postgraduate programme. During his search, he shortlisted a programme on inclusive environments, inclusive environment being a much wider term for accessible environments. He could have pursued a master's degree in any other area related to occupational therapy or rehabilitation, but he decided on inclusive environments because of the interest he had gained during the UN–ESCAP training workshop in Bangkok and our Access days. I too was looking at pursuing higher studies after the completion of my architecture technology course, and a postgraduate programme in inclusive environments was perfect for me as well. That was when I dared dream a bigger dream—of studying a subject I was passionate about in the company of my best friend.

The programme was being offered at the University of Reading in the UK. Both Vikas and I got admission to the fall session beginning in 2004. Vikas changed his job and shifted to the Royal Berkshire Hospital in Reading as they were willing to sponsor his postgraduate course. For me, however, getting admission was the only easy part. It was a whole new struggle to organize the money for tuition fees and living expenses. The amount I needed was far greater than what students usually require because I needed to take my carer along, doubling the living expenses. The dream I dreamt, it seemed, was much larger than me. But the prospect of being able to do my postgrad with Vikas was something I could not let go of—it sealed my determination not to give up. I had to be able to go for the course, no matter what.

I applied for an educational scholarship. I was hopeful about getting it because I was applying for a university programme that would equip me with the knowledge necessary for mainstreaming people with disabilities in India, and such a programme was not offered anywhere in India. My interview was held in Delhi on a hot May afternoon. I started getting anxious when I saw the number of young and bright people who had also come to be interviewed. Thankfully, my turn came quite soon and I did not have to suffer too long. There were three people on the interview panel, and they asked me several questions that I thought I answered satisfactorily. I was extremely nervous throughout—the importance of getting the scholarship was tremendous for me—but I hoped it did not show. The results were to be announced in the evening, and I returned home feeling confident about getting it—rejection was something I could not afford to even think of since I had no fall-back plan. When the results were declared, I found out that I hadn't been selected. The news shattered me.

What was I going to do now? I had no idea how was I going to manage the money. My future seemed to be ending even before its beginning.

It was then that I truly felt the power of love.

Love can be different things for different people. Love for Daddy was his religious faith and his belief that it was Sai Baba's grace which guided him. But for me love meant Vikas—and it was my love for Vikas that was my guiding force. Love is a powerful force when it is selfless and pure. True love, I believe, can give one the strength to overcome any hurdle. It was love that gave me the unwavering determination to never give up.

It is said that the entire universe works for you if you have unflinching resolve. I felt the universe working for me at that time.

After the setback of not getting the scholarship, I spent little time in mourning. I started afresh the next day, strategizing my modus operandi to make my dream come true. It was not an easy road to tread for the next four months, with far more disappointments than successes, but what helped me was reminding myself of my goal each time I failed. I got up and fought again and again, clinging to my goal. It required a lot of determination, faith and patience, but I wasn't ready to give up. Throughout, I kept telling Vikas that I was going to make it, no matter what. He found it hard to believe because he knew exactly how big a task it was for me and was aware of how hard I was trying and yet failing. But what he could not understand from our chats was the energy my determination had given me.

It was in 2004 that I received the Neerja Bhanot Award. The awarded is presented yearly to commemorate Neerja Bhanot, a real-life hero who gave up her life saving passengers on her hijacked flight. The award is given to a woman who shows exemplary courage and works for the benefit of others in spite of her own trying circumstances. It was a matter of great pride for me to receive the award in memory of such an exceptional young lady.

I went to Chandigarh to receive the award. The organizers, aware of my interest in accessibility, had most kindly arranged for a wooden ramp for me to enter the auditorium on the first floor. Unfortunately, the ramp was actually wooden planks nailed together over the staircase, and hence was dangerously steep. They had gone out of their way to provide me comfort, but I could not make use of it. I realized that there was a lot of goodwill in people to promote access for all; what was really missing was the understanding of how to provide it. The additional benefit for me was the substantial cash award that came with the felicitation. It turned out to be the beginning of my education fund.

That same year, I received the National Role Model Award, one of the awards presented annually by the Ministry of Social Justice and Empowerment, on December 3, International Day of Persons with Disabilities. The President of India gives out the award in recognition of exemplary work done by a disabled individual. I was, unfortunately, already in the UK by that time; Daddy received the award on my behalf from Dr A.P.J. Abdul Kalam.

It was only in the last month before the course started in the UK did everything finally fall into place. An education loan was sanctioned by the National Handicap Finance and Development Corporation, which gives out a soft loan to disabled people for higher studies. I also received a couple of smaller scholarships and endowments. Finally, just a week before I was to reach the UK, did Vikas believe that it was happening and start to look for accommodation for us. Sharing accommodation with Vikas was the most cost-effective option available to me—it was cheaper than living in university hostels or renting by myself. By a stroke of luck, he found a three-bedroom house in New Street, within walking distance from the university. The house had a bedroom and a bathroom on the ground floor, and two more bedrooms on the first floor. This was fantastic as in the UK one mostly finds houses with all the bedrooms and bathrooms on the first floor. Vikas negotiated the rent to fit into our budget, and everything was set. Vikas and I were going to be course mates and also housemates—this was far more than I had imagined. Reality was better than the dream.

Even today, when I think back, I believe that there was divine intervention for things to have worked out the way they did.

I reached the UK, with Ritu, on 28 August 2004. Shipra and Ajay picked us up from the airport once again; only, this time, we drove straight to Reading.

≈ ≈

By the time Ajay finally drove up to our new home, I was very excited. He parked right outside the house. The road had detached and semi-detached Victorian-style houses on both sides. Ours was probably the fifth house from the main road. There was a small entrance gate followed by a short red-tiled walkway that led to the ivory-coloured main door. There was a small garden next to the walkway. It had a red-brick facade with clinging wisteria vines and bunches of full blooms in varying shades of purple. A large Victorian window next to the main door looked out into the garden. The slanting roof was of slate, with a chimney protruding out of it. Even though the two-storeyed house looked similar to the other houses on the road, to me it was very special and unique.

As Vikas was transferring me out of the car and into my wheelchair, he had to remind me to move a couple of times— my attention was completely taken up by the house. Once I was in my chair, Vikas pushed me up the curb and onto the pavement. I hadn't uttered a word since I had seen the house—I was simply absorbing everything and realizing that this was real. When Vikas opened the gate and tipped my wheelchair over the small entrance step, I felt like a bride being carried over the threshold. This was going to be our home for the next two years!

Everyone else was busy unloading the car. Vikas joined them after leaving me in the living room. I just sat there, dazed, imbibing the house. The walls were ivory-coloured and with a granular finish. The floor had a dark grey wall-to-wall carpet. As one entered through the vestibule, my bedroom was to the right. The living room was next to it. One step down and ahead of the living room was the kitchen, followed by the washroom. The steps to the upper floor led up from the living room. While the room was small and already filled with large and comfortable blue-grey upholstered sofas, the natural light that came in through the Victorian window made it look bigger. Through the window, I could see a part of our backyard and an apple tree that bore small green apples. The thought of having apples growing in our own garden made both Ritu and me scream with delight.

How I wished Ubbu was here with us! She would have loved the sofas and the large backyard. But she was back home in India, being looked after by Daddy once again. I prepared Ubbu before I left by telling her that she had to stay in a hostel for some time, with Daddy as her warden—I had myself lived in hostels for a long time, and it was now her turn. But Ubbu, with her strong sixth sense, already knew that Ritu and I were going away and was not happy about it at all. Neither was I, actually, but I knew Daddy would take good care of her and she would be fine. It was only for a couple of years, after all.

Shipra, Ritu and Vikas worked hard to clean the house. Ajay

wasn't someone who would get involved in that task and I was hardly any help. Shipra also helped in setting up the kitchen. Being older to me, even though by a couple of months only, she took it upon herself to ensure I was comfortable and our house well-stocked. Both of us couldn't help but think of Jiya, who would have done the same. Jiya, Shipra and I had so many unforgettable childhood memories together. While Jiya spent more time with my grandmother, Shipra and I kept busy playing childish games. We were happy that we were going to get an opportunity spend a lot of time together again for such a long time.

With all her help, Shipra had proved beyond doubt that she was my family in this new country and I did not need to worry about anything. And, throughout my stay in the UK, we lived like a family, visiting each other and spending weekends together. Vikas had developed his own bond with Shipra and Ajay in the two years he had spent in the UK before my arrival, so he too was already a part of their family.

❄❄❄

The life we lived in the UK was perhaps the most beautiful time Vikas and I spent together. Both of us made our home with each other, away from the society that forced us to hide our feelings for each other from everyone. Finally, the time had come when we could express our love for each other freely. The uncomfortable feeling of losing each other under pressure from society disappeared, and we could now fully express the fact that we were much more than best friends to each other. It was a time when all that mattered to either was the other.

Our lives together couldn't have been more perfect in any

way. We were living like a couple—except, it was much better because our expectations from the other were negligible. Our being together felt so natural that it was as if it was meant to be. We, by ourselves, had never planned on being together any time in the future; but someone, somewhere seemed to have done it for us.

It wasn't long before settling into the house that Vikas declared himself 'the King of the Living Room'. He would return from work, change out of his uniform and make himself comfortable on the couch opposite the television. He would then rest for a while; my task during this time was to massage his head gently while he took his power nap. After the nap, he would sit with his laptop in front of him and simultaneously watch TV. He enjoyed reading news about the latest developments in accessibility around the world on the Internet; the television would be tuned to regular comedy shows.

Vikas taught me to laugh out loud during funny scenes on TV. Otherwise, the best I had managed thus far was only a smile at the funniest of scenes. His laughter was contagious and I could not help laughing loud. I don't recall ever hearing Daddy laugh loudly, though Mummy used to. I guess I had forgotten to laugh for a while. Just as he made me laugh during comedies, Vikas would make fun of me as I cried through tragic scenes in movies.

Within a month of my being in the UK, Vikas purchased a car. He worked out that his owning a car would be the cheapest and most convenient mode of transport for us to go sightseeing around the country. Sure enough, there were plenty of opportunities for us to go out once he bought his Red Hundai Coupe. Sometimes, he would call me from work and ask me to be ready to go for a movie right afterwards.

Oh, it was such fun! It brought back childhood memories for me, days that I had almost forgotten—the days when Mummy would get movie tickets on her way home from office and we would rush to catch the show. I was, I realized, utterly content. Life was simple yet meaningful.

Vikas and I went on numerous road trips throughout the UK. He would jokingly say to me, 'I want to make sure you see every part of the country because I don't want you to accuse me later of not letting you do so!' I had to learn to navigate, which was not as easy as it sounds for me, a person who didn't know anything about driving. The first time I tried to navigate was on a trip to London. By the time we reached, we had taken at least two wrong turns and my shoulders were aching and tight because the stress. After that, we made several other trips, from the Lake District to Wales, from the Isle of Wight to Scotland.

Ritu and I were interested in gardening, so we started to slowly clean the back lawn. Vikas often drove us to the garden shop and we bought a number of flower bulbs and also a big packet of grass seeds. I can never forget that winter day in November when Ritu and I were in the yard, trying to clean the lawn by pulling out the ivy from a small patch. We often did this as cleaning the whole yard all at once would not have been possible. It was Vikas's day off from work, so he joined us outside. He stood next to me for a while, looking at Ritu doing her work and smoking a cigarette. 'What are you doing?' he casually asked.

'Cleaning the ivy,' I responded. 'The entire yard has just this creeper. We can grow grass only once this is removed.' I was frustrated because the major portion of the yard was still to be cleaned.

It was very unlike him, but Vikas immediately went and joined Ritu in pulling out the ivy roots. Ritu was happy to have some company in performing this mundane task. Vikas's presence perked up our energies, and we decided to clean the entire lawn that day itself. Neither of us knew what the best way to do this would be, but Vikas and Ritu went ahead and started with whatever tools we had. I sat in one corner, shouting out my expert inputs.

Even after an hour, the final goal seemed far away. But Vikas's mind was made up. He wanted to finish the task now that he had started. I got tired just looking at the two of them working so hard and kept asking them to stop for the day. However, Vikas was a very headstrong man—nothing was going to deter him from achieving his goal. It was a cold day in February and it started snowing lightly. I was freezing from the cold, while both of them were sweating from hard work. I again pleaded with Vikas to stop for the day. When he didn't, I asked to be taken in out of the snow, thinking to play the 'Come on, I am disabled, take me out of the snow' card. No, that was not going to work either—for Vikas, disability had no meaning. I could pity myself but not him. Instead of stopping and taking me in, he got an umbrella from the house and fixed it to my wheelchair to keep me out of the snow while he and Ritu continued working.

All of us kept laughing at our stupidity in cleaning the lawn in the snow, but it was this very same silliness that made that day unforgettable. Such incidents made me realize that it was these small pleasures that made my life so special and memorable and continued loosening up my very straight-jacketed attitude towards life.

22

Our postgraduation was a modular course, wherein we needed to pass six modules and submit a dissertation to get a degree. Our contact days at the university were only those when the modules would run. The fee structure and schedule for a part-time student like Vikas and a full-time student like me were the same. The university generally never had full-time students for this course, but they had made an exception for me. Vikas and I therefore had our classes together, had to do the same assignments and also wrote all our examinations together. Vikas, as always, scored well in all his assignments, while I was a mediocre student.

Our fellow students were all people who were well established in their careers. Some even opted to do only one or two modules, based on their interests, for which they were given certificates of completion. Some took the modules, as and when time permitted them, over a period of five years. So there were only a few of us who did all the modules together. One such person was Julie, who worked with the city council in Wales as an interior designer. She became a good friend. Each time she travelled to Reading for the modules, she would either come to our place for dinner or we would go out together. We also travelled to Wales to visit her and her family.

We had two examinations, with three modules examined

each time. Exams were good times for us, especially the ones we had in the summers. Vikas was granted short preparatory leave from work. During the bright summer days, we sat out in our backyard, enjoying the summer breeze as we studied. Vikas sprawled on his lounge chair beside me, discussing and making notes. He was brilliant at making notes that were precise and very helpful for revisions. The only way I knew of studying, on the other hand, was mugging, which always gave me average results. My mind was forever diverted towards all things other than my books, and occasionally towards the ice-cream van that came to our street at exactly four in the afternoon. As soon as we would hear its music, we would rush out with a couple of pounds in change to buy ice-cream. This was, for me, the high point of the day—my enjoyment of these frivolous moments with Vikas. After this welcome break, with beaming smiles, we would return to our books. For Vikas, achieving distinction in his exams and assignments was easy; for me, I just about managed to pass despite putting in far more effort than him. But, then, marks didn't matter. I was studying to learn and not to excel in exams.

Higher education, according to me, is not a struggle to get great grades; instead, it is more for broadening our outlook on the subject we study. Our entire programme was designed for the British systems and laws on various aspects of creating inclusive environments—this included not only infrastructure that we were already aware of from our UN training but also areas such as access to public transport systems, housing for disabled people, communications requirements (especially for people with sensory impairments), laws for ensuring accessibility, and many other issues. Not that we could directly use this education for our work in India—what the course gave us was an understanding of what accessibility for all meant and the various aspects we needed to consider in order to improve accessibility and facilitate the societal inclusion of people with disabilities in our country. It gave us adequate understanding to be able to critique existing laws, policies, procedures and systems, and helped us improve and recommend better changes for a holistic, long-term growth for the inclusion of disabled people in the future. If I were to put it in another way, I would say that while the UN training in Bangkok made accessibility an issue we were passionate about, our postgraduate course gave us direction in terms of how we could give concrete shape to it to make accessibility our profession as well.

The most important thing that our education gave us was the opportunity to learn together, which allowed us both to be in sync with each other in the way our minds functioned. Formulating a certain way of approaching the issue helped us in our future work together—we were able to discuss ideas and concepts at a much deeper level, making our output more meaningful and valuable.

Call it the force of circumstances or whatever, but we were the only two people from India in those days to be fortunate to have had that kind of training in accessibility. More importantly, we were the only ones with that level of understanding of accessibility and a sense of value for our work. The reason for our in-depth understanding, of course, was not limited to the education we received; it was a result of many factors, ranging from my being a disabled person and having first-hand experience, to Vikas having a rehabilitation background.

I can never emphasize this enough: Vikas and I were a team. It was our education together that laid the foundation for the organization we would set up in the future, and gave us the power to think differently and to not accept things as they had always been. It gave us the courage to stand up for what we believed in. AccessAbility, our organization, was an outcome of this.

23

My return to India after the course was not easy for either of us. Again it seemed like the end of the road for our relationship—there was nothing else I could do for us to be together any longer. It was, yet again, that horrible feeling of parting—only, much worse. As much as we would have liked time to freeze, it just kept ticking onwards. I could not feel happy thinking of the future when there was no hope of our being together.

On my last day in Reading, Vikas helped Ritu to pack my bags. I felt like there was a lump lodged in my throat. I couldn't help but say to Vikas: 'If you do not have the choice to marry me, then you have the choice of not marrying at all.'

I started crying. Vikas just hugged me for a long time, without uttering a word. Then he bent down to kiss me on my forehead. This was the first time in all these years that we had acknowledged our desire to marry each other.

I sniffed and continued speaking: 'I don't blame your parents, but I wish they had rejected our affection for each other after knowing me as a person.' But both of us knew how useless my words were—how what we felt for each other didn't matter to anyone else.

Shipra and Ajay came that evening. They were going to see me off at the airport.

Quite late in the evening, only about nine hours before we

were to leave for the airport, Ritu suddenly said that she wanted to carry a thick jacket for her father to wear when he worked at his farm on early winter mornings. There was no point in telling her that she had come up too late with her request; since we were not going to return to the UK, she might as well buy what she wanted. Vikas drove us to a supermarket to select something from the clothing selection. It was refreshing to get out of the house then as putting up a strong and emotionless façade in front of everyone who had come to bid me farewell was nearly strangulating me.

As Ritu strolled around the store, looking at the numerous jackets on display, Vikas and I had a few quiet moments to ourselves, enveloped by clothes racks. We lingered with each for what seemed like eternity. There were tears in our eyes. This was the end.

Vikas took my hand in his and gently said, 'I love you.' I knew it came straight from his heart.

We kissed goodbye there, in the middle of the supermarket, surrounded by a protective canopy of clothes on all sides. I had never felt this kind of pain before.

≈≈≈

Vikas shifted back to the hospital accommodation after Ritu and I returned. He hated living there alone, but he had no choice. Unwillingly, he went back to his one-room existence, lonely, surviving on instant food, television and the computer.

Back in Delhi, by January 2006, I shifted back into my own house in Vasant Kunj after being away for four years. It seemed like only yesterday to me when Vikas and I had spent our evenings together with friends. It felt as though it was just recently that Vikas had got Ubbu, who was now four years old. There were so many memories that this house had stored in itself!

Ubbu was probably the only one to be excited and happy at that time because she had Ritu and me back. She, of course, moved in with me. As expected, she had been very mischievous and troubled Daddy a lot while I was away. But Daddy had never complained and always had his arms open for my crazy dog. Daddy and Meera were finally living together in Faridabad in the house my grandparents had left for Daddy, and I was very happy for them.

I kept thoughts about missing the UK and being with Vikas out of my mind; I concentrated instead on looking forward to my new job assignment, which was to begin in February.

I joined a big corporate house in Delhi as the programme manager of their corporate social responsibility programme. My job entailed setting up the programme, and they were keen to work towards improving accessibility for people with disabilities in India. This was the perfect job profile for me— their goal appeared to be the same as mine. I worked well for about six months, after which I started facing human resource issues. They arose out of the rigidity of the HR department, and their inability to appreciate my special needs.

When I joined, the managing director, who was my direct boss, was not in the country. The building where my office was located had an inaccessible main entrance and had about ten or twelve steps. There was an accessible entrance, but that was for VIPs only. For two months—that is, until my boss returned to office—I was carried up on my wheelchair to the office. In spite of regular requests to HR to give me permission to use the VIP entrance, the vice-president of the department of such a big company appeared not to have the power to allow me to use the VIP entrance. It was a shameful start, especially because I was supposed to be a proponent of accessibility. But being the person that I am—and in the hope of being able to fight larger discrimination from my position at work—I did not retaliate and just let it pass. It was only when the MD returned that I got permission to enter the office with the dignity and ease that I deserved. What took me time to realize was that there were no bigger discriminations that I could fight for unless I fought for myself. Without fighting for my own rights, there was no way I could fight for anyone else's.

Similar discriminations continued. Eventually, after ten months of work, I had to resign. It wasn't easy for me to decide to quit. It took a lot of ill-treatment for me to finally take such a drastic step. I had a large educational loan to be repaid, and without the job I had no source of income. But I realized that there was no point in continuing to work with the organization as there was nothing I could really achieve by staying on given the kind of attitude the company had towards its one and only disabled employee. I dedicated everything I had to my cause, so money was little incentive to stay back.

My experience was not unique. It was a typical example of the kind of discrimination disabled people face every day. The discrimination is often very subtle, and many a time it makes us feel that we are being unreasonable by asking for our rights. As in my case, companies are unable or unwilling to make any accommodations for retaining a disabled employee. Even though they may not get another person as qualified, experienced and with a passion for the job, it is easier for them to let the disabled employee go. My abilities were not appreciated; rather, my disability was made an issue of.

I consoled myself by saying that I was just not cut out for a corporate job with a straight action plan to be followed and without much risk or challenge. Also, I believe that I was far too strong and individualistic in my attitude by then to merge quietly into the system. However, I was angry about the way I was treated. I felt very let down, considering how much I had contributed to the organization in my ten months there. I actually set up their department and gave it direction. Sure, they paid me for my services, but it wasn't solely money that I was working for. I think anybody who is like me—a person who works for personal satisfaction and not only for money—would have been hurt in a similar situation. Thankfully, Vikas was in India for a long holiday when all of this happened. He was just as angry about the way his friend had been treated. That common anger directed us to fight and bring about change in society.

Vikas and I had invested a lot of time and resources to make us the best in our field. It was time to make a strong appearance and reap the benefits of our investment. Along with our old friend Sachin, we formed AccessAbility, our own organization.

※※※

While our area of work was the promotion of inclusive environments, our fight was as much against charity and unprofessionalism in the disability sector. We were frustrated by the deep roots that charity had taken in the disability sector, wherein most non-governmental and governmental organizations considered making provisions for the disabled as 'God's work', jeopardizing any chance of real inclusion. We set out to bring change within the sector as well as outside the sector. The last thing that a disabled person wants is charity, and we wanted to weed it out. We had the enthusiasm, skills and qualifications—there was nothing to pull us back. We hoped to create a society in which disability is looked at as a mainstream developmental issue rather than a charitable one.

It didn't take us long to set up. We were operational in less than a month from my resignation. Our office: the round dining table at my house. Every day, the three of us sat at my dining table, thinking about AccessAbility till late into the night. Even arriving at the name took a lot of thinking. AccessAbility, according to us, translated as 'Access = Ability'. We were so fuelled with unfulfilled dreams, plans and ideas that they easily translated into social entrepreneurship. AccessAbility was running through our veins, it was alive—we were 'access nerds'. All we could talk about was our work, our minds were consumed by our work, and we drew pleasure from our work! There seemed to be nothing else for us except the cause and our work.

As the first step in our fight, we decided to form AccessAbility as a firm rather than a non-governmental organization. Our reasoning was simple: we believed that we could not fight charity if we ourselves were dependent on it. This was very different from our thinking a few years ago when we had formed Access—then we had looked at doing projects that got funded but not the projects we really wanted to do. Now we were sure that we wanted to do everything our way. We were not willing to accept restrictions, boundaries and limitations. Our work had to be performed freely.

We adopted a purely business model—something that is rare in disability-related work in India. Considering that disability is still not a mainstream issue, we were way ahead of our time trying to run our organization as a business. But we strongly believed in our model. We believed that responsible service providers and employers would recognize the long-term social, ethical and business mileage in valuing their disabled clients and employees, and would therefore be willing to invest in making provisions for them. We sustained ourselves by charging a fee for the professional service that we provided to companies and employers looking at making their service or workplace more inclusive.

Contrary to common practice, we set out to change the world, not the disabled person who is expected to fit in with and adapt to the world. Our clients were business houses, not people with disabilities who were the beneficiaries of our work. We took pride in calling ourselves the only professional organization in the disability sector. When I say 'professional', I do not only reflect on the high standards of output we delivered to our clients but also on the fact that we were providing this service after educating ourselves adequately to do so. This itself was uncommon in India: having a generous heart, a patient disposition, good connections and some kind of exposure is usually considered sufficient qualification to work in the sector.

Vikas took a two-year-long break from his permanent residency and returned to India in September 2007. He would have done anything to move back to India, especially because he knew that I wouldn't shift to the UK. In these two years, he wanted to give AccessAbility a fair chance and see if he could move back for good.

By then, a year had passed since we started AccessAbility. On his return, Vikas immediately joined as a full-time partner after being a remote partner supporting us via the Internet. Sachin and I had, in this year, got into a regular working system, and because of the workload we didn't have the time to discuss ideas and strategies as much as we used to when we had started. It was with Vikas's return that we once again became access nerds, talking-walking-thinking-drinking-eating accessibility. His return rejuvenated us and we quickly expanded manifold. We shifted to a larger office, expanded our work and got a larger team.

It wasn't long before our way of thinking and approaching the issue of accessibility was known throughout India. We bagged good private sector clients in the hospitality, retail, education and healthcare industries. We were making very good progress in spite of being forerunners in what we did. One of our best clients, for whom we did the maximum work, was ITC's hotel division. We worked with their team to make each and every hotel property they owned more comfortable for disabled and elderly guests. We also authored two books for them: a short handbook called *Employing Persons with Disabilities*, and a technical book with design standards for hotel accessibility called *A Guide to Universal Design in Built Environments*.

We were fortunate that the work accomplished by AccessAbility got recognition in prestigious quarters. The disability sector has two significant awards and I, in recognition of our work, received both of these: the Ability Award and the NCEPDP Shell-Helen Keller Award. At every opportunity, I knew at all times that it couldn't have been possible without a team effort.

Our work also attracted regular coverage in both print and electronic media. We were making sharp progress each day, gaining recognition nationally as well as internationally.

We built on our knowledge with each assignment, exerting ourselves and improving professionally. It was the opportunity for self-improvement and knowledge increment that pushed us further. We did not mind ploughing most of our earnings back into our business because we were sure of succeeding.

We were happy because we had created something we were all very proud of. We were living our dream and doing what we felt passionate about, and in the manner we deemed fit. There was nothing that could stop us now. We had taken off!

Book 4

Gaining Acceptance

24

On 13 January 2009, northern India was celebrating Lori. While in rural India farmers celebrate their harvest, in the cities it is an occasion to get together, have a bonfire and celebrate. That morning, Vikas said, 'Let's have a party.'

Vikas had been in India since September 2007 and was scheduled to return to the UK in September 2009. He was, as always, full of life and possessed an unsurpassable energy to both work and party. His days were still long and ended way past midnight as there was always so much he wanted to do. Not once in the ten years that I had known him did I hear him say that he was bored. His mind remained sharp, no matter what time of the day, and he loved celebrating life and would let no occasion to do so pass. Through the course of our long relationship, he had managed pull me along—he instilled in me the energy to have long days like him and be involved in various things simultaneously, whether they were work-related or for fun. I was the one who had to host the countless parties he wanted to have.

At our AccessAbility office, Vikas said, 'Let's have a bonfire and a barbeque today.' As always, it stressed me out to think about making all the arrangements. But I responded as expected: 'That a great idea!' I was hoping that today would be a bit different as it was a barbeque and I didn't need to cook food. For a change, I thought with a satisfied smirk on my face, I would eat while others cooked. Vikas had very recently been gifted the barbeque by Mamaji, his favourite maternal uncle. This was the first time we were going to try using it. 'We won't need any dinner after the barbeque, right?' I enquired hopefully.

'Oh, no! Cook some mutton curry, and we'll order naans from a takeaway. People leaving towards the end always like to eat,' replied Vikas.

So there I was, having to ensure that some home-cooked mutton curry was ready—for the millionth time. I was wheeling around tensely, ordering kebabs for the barbeque and mutton to cook, cold drinks and namkeens to nibble on with the drinks. Thank God for home delivery in my locality, otherwise it would have been far more difficult!

I was an anxious person those days. I didn't really need to be tense as Vikas and Ritu were there to help, but I just seemed to enjoy bearing the entire responsibility for the party and everything else. It made me feel worthwhile and important, I guess. I wanted everything to be perfect. I wanted to be a great hostess. I wanted Vikas to be happy and proud. I wanted to be a part of all the preparations instead of being an onlooker. I would have tension-knots in my stomach from all this wanting. No amount of organization practice thanks to all the parties we had made it easier for me.

I suppose the tension resulted from the fact that I could not really do anything myself. I needed help, and mostly the help was from Ritu. I would wheel myself around, telling Ritu things like 'Cut the onions and put it on the burner with the meat, I'll supervise it and you can clean up in the meantime.' Ritu had been with me for over eight years and helped me host countless parties. By now, she knew the drill and liked to do things at her own pace and style. Cleaning was always her priority. She would invariably like to finish cleaning before cooking. Working simultaneously on two chores did not sit well with her. Moreover, she could manage it all herself and did not need my help or instruction.

Her relaxed attitude would make me even more anxious, to the extent that I would actually need to lie down and loosen up. Often I managed to rub off my tension on her; we'd both then fight. At other times, knowing my nature well, she'd play along, keeping me busy stirring the mutton on the burner while she cleaned.

As we lit the barbeque, the air was filled with smoke. Soon it subsided and was replaced by the delicious smell of kebabs. Ubbu, who was by now seven years old, had her nose working overtime, tickled as it was by the aroma of the kebabs. She stood next to the barbeque table, waiting patiently for her share. Her brown eyes were mournful from trying to ensure that she was not forgotten.

We had a bonfire in the middle of the park in front of our house. The park was just mud, with no traces of grass. The only greenery was a couple of trees and a small green patch maintained by me. We put the barbeque and all ingredients on a table outside on the walking path in front of the house. This section of the path was used only by us, so this did not disturb anyone. The latest in hip-hop bellowed through the windows from the music system. We pulled out chairs from inside the house and sat around the bonfire, putting popcorn and ravari into the fire, which was the customary thing to do on Lori. The drinks were being served inside the house, so the only time one needed to go into the house was to replenish one's glass. It was a lovely evening, and everyone was happy after a couple of drinks.

The party wound up around 1 a.m. Ritu was clearing up in the kitchen and Ubbu was fishing through the bins for bones. Exhausted and wasted at the end of the day, Vikas flopped on a chair around the round dining table. Vishal, Vikas's younger brother, flopped on another chair. I had known Vishal for about four years now and we were good friends. Vishal had even stayed with us for a couple of months in the UK.

Vishal and I knew just how Vikas came alive as the evening drew closer. Vishal often joined us at my house since Vikas's return from the UK, and the three of us sat around the dining table, drinking whisky, eating snacks and watching a movie. It was our favourite pastime. Vikas would sit in his favourite place, which was where one felt the maximum blast from the air-conditioning and had a good view of the television. Here, in India, too he was the King of the Living Room. He always had his laptop in front of him and a cigarette in his hand. Vishal always did as his brother asked him to, and was designated bartender. Nothing in the world could move Vikas once he was seated on his throne, and he felt he had every right to make his younger brother run around doing the tasks he didn't want to do himself.

My job was to keep the snacks coming and to have dinner ready. So my designated place at the table was next to the kitchen. Vikas disliked my spending time in the kitchen, but all the same I liked to cook for him and regularly did so. All he wanted me to cook, though, was non-vegetarian curry or biryani. He didn't enjoy eating vegetarian for dinner, so I didn't have too many options. Deciding the menu was easy. It was mostly chicken or mutton curry—no fish, as I didn't know how to cook fish. Ritu's evenings were spent in the kitchen, getting dinner ready. I often supervised her, but she was a great cook by now.

As the evening progressed, Vikas would become fresher and livelier. His eyes would start to sparkle. Invariably, just as the movie would reach its climax, Vikas would draw our attention to some issue pertaining to disability—whether it was the disability law and its loopholes or the lack of accessibility in public places or just discussing the difference between inclusion and mainstreaming. Both Vishal and I would clench our eyes and think to ourselves: 'Oh, no! Not again!'

'Vikas, please!' I would plead. 'Let's discuss this after the movie is over.' But he was unstoppable. This was one of the few occasions when he would jump out of his throne and put the movie on pause so he could have my undivided attention. Vishal, poor fellow, who had no interest in disability or its politics, had to quietly endure it. This, I guess, was the price he had to pay for a good evening with his brother.

We would watch the rest of the movie with breaks depending on Vikas. He was very brilliant and all of us who knew him well thought that he should have been a lawyer. I—the person whom disability affected the most—was lukewarm in discussing these issues out of office hours; for Vikas, it was a passion.

By the end of our Lori party, Vishal had had a drink too many and it was hard for me to understand a word of what he was trying to say. Vikas kept telling him to shut up and leave; Vishal kept saying 'Tell her!' again and again, growing more emphatic by the minute. By now I had guessed that the tension between the two brothers involved me. My curiosity was growing. What must Vikas tell me that he didn't want to? 'Tell me what?' I finally asked. Vikas answered: 'Nothing.' This went on for some time until, finally, he said, 'My parents have agreed for my marriage.'

My heart skipped a beat as I heard him say that. I had known that this would come up some day, but I wasn't ready for it today. Maybe I would not have been ready for it any day. I didn't want to hear any more—I loved Vikas far too much.

'Agreed to your marriage, that's good! Who are you getting married to?' I finally said, mustering all my courage.

'My parents have agreed for me to get married to you,' Vikas replied.

'What?' I said in astonishment, convinced that I hadn't heard him right.

'My parents have agreed for me to get married to you,' Vikas repeated in a calm and composed manner.

There was a long silence. I did not know how to react and my brain felt numb. I was finding it difficult to comprehend what he was saying. There was a surge of thoughts, emotions and questions suddenly reeling in my mind, but I just sat there in shocked in silence, not knowing what to say. I could not understand how Vikas was so cool about this and hadn't wanted to tell me. Besides, I wasn't going to discuss all this in front of Vishal.

The two brothers left while I simply sat there, dazed. I did not utter another word that evening. I went to bed in a state of shock and slept a dreamless sleep.

After making myself believe for ten years that there would be no marriage, this was not something I was prepared for. I would probably have had a more spontaneous response had Vikas told me the name of some other girl he was planning to marry! I was feeling something close to what I had felt after our first kiss—confused and scared. I didn't know what was going to happen next and what the future held for me.

Things between me and Vikas's parents hadn't gone right from the beginning. Not that we had ever met formally to discuss anything or even argued with them. It was simply understood that I was not going to be the one Vikas was going to marry. I had met them only once, long ago, when Vikas had just joined the spinal centre. All these years, they had been aware of my existence and importance in Vikas's life, but had probably hoped that Vikas would see better sense finally and decide to move on. I couldn't really blame them for not accepting me—any parent would want the best for their child, and I knew I wasn't the best Vikas could get.

Over time, Vikas had started spending very little time with his parents and had stopped meeting his close family altogether, spending all his time with me instead. It was as if he was running away from his family, unable to share his heart with them. But I never intervened in his relationship with his parents.

Now, after all these years, for his parents to suddenly accept our relationship seemed strange to me, and difficult to believe. We had been through so much together—marriage, somehow, had begun to seem unimportant by now. After our closeness through all these years, what did marriage really mean? How would it change our lives? After having hidden our love from the world, the idea of suddenly proclaiming it to everyone seemed odd. I didn't know if it was even necessary. I simply wasn't prepared for it.

Vikas and I did not speak about this for a week. In fact, I did not speak to anyone about it. The gravity of what Vikas had said had still not sunk in. I went through the week normally, just a bit withdrawn, thinking mostly about the past and the future. Vikas was just as normal. We were together each day from morning till night, as always, but both of us pretended as though nothing had happened. We were experts at pretending by now. I did not meet Vishal for a while after that evening, though. I found out later that the brothers had fought on their way home from the party—Vikas was very cross at Vishal for spilling the beans.

Though I could not yet reconcile myself to the idea of marriage, strangely enough, the proposition seemed to heal me somewhere within and bring back my faith in life. It seemed to calm the anger I had felt towards society since my accident. It was bizarre, I realized, but somehow, the thought of getting married seem to wash away all my negative disability karma. Marriage, at that moment, was symbolic of society accepting me as I was, with all my shortcomings—just the way Vikas accepted me. I knew this was a result of his long but silent fight with his family to get me the acceptance I deserved, and I felt grateful for it.

✳

In the week following Lori, Jiya came to Delhi on a work trip. Daddy and Meera also came over to my place to be able to spend time with Jiya as her trips to Delhi were rare and short. One evening, we were invited to Asha Bua's house for dinner, and I had called the driver to take us there. It was the end of January now, and the cold had lessened. We left home at about seven in the evening and stopped at the local market to buy some flowers for Asha Bua. As always, I sat next to the driver in the front seat, and Jiya, Daddy and Meera sat in the back.

As soon as we drove out of our colony gate, I announced, 'Vikas's parents have agreed to our marriage.' I just could not keep it to myself any longer.

'Wow, that's excellent!' was the unanimous response from the backseat. Nothing more than that! I had taken them all by surprise. They were all aware of my close friendship with Vikas, but, like me, had never anticipated our marriage. The rest of the journey was spent in silence to my disappointment. I was ready to talk about it, but I guess all of them were in the same state of shock as I had been a few days ago. The dinner at Asha Bua's place went as usual and not a word was spoken about my marriage. I began to think that no one was taking me seriously because they thought it was not possible.

I was not seeking permission from anyone. But I was trying to understand the situation better by sharing. Also, I was concerned about Vikas having to live with my disability. I could not help but be disappointed by my family's lack of reaction.

It was the next day that Jiya came to speak to me. She was coping with marital issues herself and negative thoughts were hovering in her mind. 'What have you thought, Chots?' she asked me. When I did not answer, she said, 'I think you should go for it. In life, companionship is extremely important.' She had carefully chosen not to use the word 'love', I noticed. But companionship was not an issue I was struggling with as Vikas was always around. My issue was the acceptance of our love by the world. However, Jiya's endorsement meant a lot to me as she had been more mother than sister to me since my accident.

Once Jiya left, Vikas and I were back to sitting around my dining table till late in the night. One evening, I nervously decided broach the topic. Nearly two weeks had passed since the Lori night, so it was rather awkward and there were butterflies fluttering in my stomach. 'Your parents have agreed—is that true?'

Vikas stopped working on his computer and looked straight into my eyes. 'Yes,' he said.

'So, what have you decided?' I asked, staring into his sparkling eyes with their long lashes.

'I don't know. What do you say?' he replied.

'Why haven't you talked about it with me after Lori?' I asked him, a hint of annoyance in my voice.

'I was waiting for you to bring it up,' he said. With that, I went back to watching the TV and Vikas went back to his computer.

'This is unbelievable!' I said after a while, nodding my head, still facing the television. 'Why have they agreed now, after all this time?' I felt a great deal of sadness for having lost so many years.

'I don't know,' said Vikas. 'They probably just want me to get married now and are fed up of me showing no interest in any other girl.'

He then told me that his parents had agreed a couple of months ago and had been after his life to make them meet me, but he had been delaying it.

'Why didn't you tell me sooner?' I asked.

'I didn't think you'd agree,' he responded.

'But I agree!'

There was no question of refusing Vikas now, when I had never refused him anything else before.

The idea of marrying Vikas, after having spent what seemed like a lifetime in constant fear of losing him, was a mixture of a dream coming true, a renewed feeling of self-respect, the bliss of being accepted by others and immeasurable happiness. It seemed to heal me within from all the pain and hurt I had ever felt. It brought me a sense of peace and serenity.

That evening, once Vikas had left, I told Ritu about our decision to get married. After a few moments of shock, she was hysterical with happiness. She threw herself at me and lay her head in my lap like a little child. Tears of joy rolled down our cheeks. We sat there for some time, enjoying the moment. It felt as though both of us were fluttering with gladness. I don't think anybody else I knew was as happy as Ritu about the marriage. I am not sure why it was so. Perhaps it was because she had been witness to and a part of us for eight years now.

Neither Ritu nor I could sleep that night and just kept babbling in a bewildered manner and making plans for the future. For years, I had asked her, 'When will I be happy?' We finally had an answer—we knew that the happy days were finally here to stay.

25

Once we decided we wanted to be wed, the first person we wanted to tell was my father. Daddy was going to Pune to be with Jiya for a month. He was going to spend a night with me and go to the airport from my house. That seemed to be the perfect evening to tell him.

I returned early from office to be with Daddy. Vikas too drove to my place straight from office as we had decided to break the news to him together. After a cup to tea and some small talk, we told him that we had decided to get married. We told him this as he was watching Barack Obama being sworn in as President of the United States on TV. Daddy knew I loved Vikas and had seen me in pain each time he left after his vacation in India. He had been fearful about the day when Vikas would leave me and marry someone else. Now, since that was never going to happen, I was sure that he would feel euphoric and support me in my decision.

But reality did not turn out the way I expected. Daddy turned his attention from the TV towards us for a short moment and, with a big smile, said, 'Congratulations, that's really nice,' and returned to the TV. This was a big moment for me and I wanted him to say more. I waited a while for some more reaction—excitement, anger, anything!—but did not get anything else out of him.

Vikas and I looked at each other, disappointed. Obama, I could not help feeling, had somehow robbed me of one of the happiest moments of my life, and Vikas was a bit offended. I consoled Vikas, trying to save face, by saying that Daddy never had an opinion of his own. He would soon be excited when he absorbed the excitement of the family. But somehow that never actually happened. I never knew or understood why he was not happy for me to get married, but it made me very sad.

At the end of the day, I had a very deep and strong bond with Daddy and he had supported me all through except in this. I always thought he was the best father in the world because of the way he took care of me and supported me. But now it seemed something had changed. What or why, I do not know, and I live with not knowing what wrong I did in marrying.

Daddy left the next morning and I went ahead with my wedding preparations by myself. However, I knew Daddy was with me in praying for my wellbeing.

It wasn't only Daddy. When I look back, I don't see any of my family members being happy in the real sense for me. Of course, nobody ever voiced that sentiment, but there was no excitement whatsoever. Maybe it was so because I had lived alone for so long and everybody was busy in their own lives, with little interaction on a regular basis. There just wasn't the kind of enthusiasm from my family that I was expecting. In spite of this, however, my excitement about the wedding did not diminish in any way. It was something that was meant to be and had been delayed enough.

Vikas kept postponing my meeting with his parents. He was not sure if his parents had agreed out of not having any other option, or if they were really happy about him marrying to me.

He did not want any compromise for anybody since the two of us could continue to live the way we had been without being married at all. After a lot of persuasion, from me as well as from them, he finally brought his parents over.

The Sunday Vikas got them to visit, he gave me precisely ten minutes to get ready. He called me in the morning and said, 'You want to meet my parents. We'll be there in ten minutes.' I begged him for more time as I was a mess and so was the house, and I definitely wanted to make the right first impression. But ten minutes it was. In a flurry, Ritu and I dumped all the extra stuff lying out of place around the house into cupboards. I quickly changed from shorts into trousers and a nice T-shirt. Ten minutes—and they reached. Thankfully, both the house and I were presentable by then.

First impressions are important for me. I wanted this meeting to go well. As the doorbell rang, Ubbu started barking. Ritu opened the door, holding on to Ubbu's chain, while I sat further inside. Ubbu was excited to see new people and happily wagged her tail and greeted them; she was then chained to my wheelchair so that she wouldn't jump at them to exhibit her love. Ritu got busy serving tea and snacks, and the rest of us settled ourselves in the living room.

There was a strange awkwardness that all of us seemed to be feeling. But Vikas's mother managed to break the ice and take things further. I guess the awkwardness was partly due to the fact that I was alone and there was no other family member around. The entire situation was very unconventional in every way.

It was a short visit. Heaven knows what they made of me, but my first impression of them was that they were very simple folk. Vikas's mother was a warm and talkative lady dressed in a cotton salwar suit. After she entered, she walked up to me and gave me a very warm hug. I was not used to being hugged so lovingly—it was always a 'Hi' or a 'Namaste' in my family. Her hug made me comfortable immediately. Vikas's father, on the other hand, seemed a little uncomfortable and hardly spoke. I guess he took time to open up to people. He just sat there with a smile on his face. I finally knew from where Vikas had inherited his smile.

His mother talked non-stop about how they had finally consented to our marriage. They were helpless, she said. Their son did not spend any time at home and they were worried about him driving back every night at 3 a.m. I knew instantly why Vikas had been hesitating about this meeting. I couldn't help but feel like the culprit who had put them through so much. All I could say was, 'Sorry, I did not want it that way,' knowing full well that it was not my fault. I knew that much of the distance between parents and son was because Vikas felt that they cared more about what society would say than their own son's feelings. He loved them immensely all the same, else he would never have waited for their permission. I saw then how difficult the growing distance must have been for all of them all these years.

Vikas was in very high spirits when he returned after dropping his parents home. It seemed as if a load had lifted off him. I had never seen him so relaxed before. Bursting with excitement, he said to me, 'Be ready for a lot of family socializing now. Our family is a Punjabi tabbar'—a large, close-knit family. It felt as though he had wanted this acceptance for very long and was finally at peace. I smiled and told him not to worry: 'I am happy to have a family after so many years of being alone.' It would be my privilege to become a part of his family.

Marriage preparations began late February. It was to be a low-key wedding at the temple, but Vikas and I were keen on a big reception. It was going to be our day of announcing our love publicly, and we wanted to celebrate it with all our friends, associates and family.

※※

Now that everything had been decided, Vikas was extremely excited. We had hidden our feelings for each other from the world for ten years, and now we wanted to shout out to the world what we felt.

The first thing that he did was to switch on his computer at the office and change his Facebook relationship status from 'Single' to 'In a relationship'; then he did the same with my account. He then waited for Sachin to arrive. Sachin generally checked his Facebook account as the first task in office every morning. Vikas just sat there, waiting patiently for him to turn on his computer, and was a bit disappointed when he did not go to Facebook immediately. He could wait no longer, and asked Sachin to check out Facebook. Sachin did, and noticed the relationship status change. 'Oh! That's nice.' He smiled sheepishly. 'But I always knew there is something going on between you guys. Good you made it public!' That was the end of the matter.

This was just not the reaction Vikas was hoping for. He went back to his work dejected, his head resting on his hand, his lower lip pouting as he sulked. He looked like a child who had not got what he wanted. He seemed to be behaving like one too! We communicated with gestures and Google chat in spite of sitting next to each other—we did that often at work, whenever we wanted to talk about something in private. I asked him to change the status to 'Engaged'—that would make a better impact. We hardly worked that day. We were just too excited and wanted to tell Sachin, who did not sense anything unusual. Finally, before Vikas became absolutely frustrated by Sachin's lack of curiosity, I announced that we had decided to get married.

We had told one friend; now there was less shyness about informing other friends. By the end of it, we became used to and confident about the fact that we were getting married.

Vikas decided that we needed go out and celebrate the good news with friends. One evening soon after this, we invited friends over to a pub to share with them our news and happiness. Four tables were combined to accommodate our large group. Everyone was very happy that we were finally going to be wed. They had all suspected something between us forever, and now the wedding announcement was a pleasant affirmation for them. As the loud music blared in the pub, we enjoyed our drinks and talked.

Suddenly, Vikas got a call from home. His maternal uncle, Mamaji, was visiting with his wife, Mamiji. On hearing the news of Vikas's marriage, he was ecstatic. It is said that when Vikas was born, on getting the news, Mamaji had jumped with happiness from the first floor and run to the hospital to see his firstborn nephew. And now that his favourite nephew was getting married, his happiness overflowed.

Vikas had for years now avoided family gatherings because invariably the issue of his marriage came up and he was sure that if he ever got married it would be only to me. Now that it was actually happening, he wanted to share each bit of his happiness as much with his family as with his friends. He asked me to come out for a moment and told me that we had to go to his house to meet Mamaji. I was suddenly very nervous. I never went to anyone's house, except Daddy and Asha Bua's; everyone always came to my house to visit. My first reaction was to say no, I didn't want to go; but I knew how much Vikas wanted this, and to refuse would seem like arrogance rather than nervousness.

I felt completely unprepared, but Vikas already had it all planned out. All our friends were going to accompany us, as they were required to help in carrying me up to Vikas's first-floor apartment. He also told me that if Mamaji approved of me then he'd make sure that the whole family accepted me. I wasn't dressed right to go to his house for the first time, especially now that I was his bride-to-be. I was wearing an old pair of jeans with a black high-neck top and a fleece jacket—definitely not the outfit I would have liked to meet his parents and Mamaji in. But I didn't have an option.

We reached Vikas's house at about 10 p.m. As decided, I was carried up with my wheelchair. It was an embarrassing moment for me—imagine the bride-to-be being carried up to her husband's home in such a manner. But it was best not to think about it. After all, this was what they had accepted in agreeing to our marriage.

Vikas hugged Mamaji as he entered. He was extremely happy to see Vikas, and pleasant yet a bit awkward with me, which was to be expected.

The flat had a large living room with seating lacing all the walls and two coffee tables placed in the centre. There was a framed pencil sketch of Vikas, which he had got made in Italy, hanging on one of the walls. At the extreme end of the room was a TV placed in front of a showcase that was set in the wall.

I instantly recognized the two stuffed toys that lay in front of the TV. I was seeing them after ten years, but they brought a smile to my face and made me feel at home. We had purchased these in Bangkok, while attending the UN training course. Just seeing them brought back memories of the Bangkok trip. It was there that Vikas had promised to be with me even when I was old and had white hair and false teeth.

My attention returned to the present as Vikas's mother offered me tea. There was no space in their living room where I could park my wheelchair properly, so I sat quite awkwardly in front of a chair, trying not to block the way. Vikas's mother and Mamiji remained busy in the kitchen, cooking for the ten unexpected guests who had just walked in. All the men got busy drinking whisky pegs. It was a big day, and Vikas's father had opened a Glenfiddich bottle to celebrate. It was one of the many bottles he had in his stock—Vikas carried one for his father each time he came to India from the UK. While the men drank, the women were given the option of masala tea followed by piping-hot instant-mix tomato soup.

I was, without doubt, the most awkward person in the crowd. I sat put in my chair, unable to help Vikas's mom in the kitchen—it is customary for daughters-in-law to help their mothers-in-law in the kitchen and in serving guests to show their interest in the household. And I just sat there, being served. Of course, no one was expecting anything from me, but it was my own sense of worthlessness that made me feel awkward. Vikas was far too occupied celebrating with Mamiji to notice my discomfort.

Vikas's mother and Mamiji cooked and served simultaneously, alternating between the kitchen and the living room, talking to all our friends. They were both perfect hostesses who could manage everything together. They had dinner ready within an hour. The men, by then, were four pegs down. Vikas, who had had drinks at the pub already, was quite happy by now. He rarely got drunk, but this was one of those few occasions when he could just not stop himself.

Everyone was finally ready to eat by midnight. The dinner spread was lavish, with more than ten dishes on the table. Just tasting each dish once would have been enough food for me. Vikas pushed my chair till the dining table in the next room as there wasn't enough space in the corridor to manoeuvre myself. Being pushed right now lowered my self-worth further. The worst was when everyone stood around holding their dinner plates and serving themselves; I needed to sit in the corner so that I could use place my plate on the table and be served.

By the time we were ready to leave, which was about 1 a.m., Vikas was far too drunk to help in carrying me down and driving me back home. I was angry with him for his carelessness. This was the first time I had come to his house, and I was upset that he did not look after me or even bother to show me around the house. This was the first time I was thinking like a wife— it wouldn't have mattered or been expected if we were just friends. Suddenly, I expected something from him. I seemed to be developing a feeling of being in his protection—after all, he was going to be my husband. The next day, I mentioned my discontent to Vikas. He heard me out and promised to take care and never repeat it.

As the day of the wedding drew closer, I began to feel utterly unsupported. I had no family to share my joy or distress with. No one I could seek advice or help from in shopping for my wedding dress and jewellery, on how to arrange the mehendi night or get the wedding cards printed, or even to tell me what gifts should traditionally go to Vikas and his family. I had no idea what was 'customary' and there was no one to guide me. I was all alone in preparing for my wedding—something that, in India, is always done for the bride by her family. I felt absolutely alone during what should have been the happiest 'family moments' of my life. Of course, I always had Vikas by my side; but this was the one time I needed my own family around me. I missed my mother terribly.

Jiya was the only one who had been in constant touch with me over the phone, but no matter how hard she tried she couldn't have been with me sooner than just a week to the wedding. Her arrival with my niece and nephew ended my anxiety, and my empty house began to shape up like a wedding house. Jiya took over all the last-moment preparations as soon as she arrived. I was finally relieved of the responsibility of organizing my own wedding.

26

We were married on 13 April 2009. It was Baisakhi, and a very auspicious day. It was a beautiful crisp April morning, a morning that both of us had dreamt of. Getting married to your best friend is as good as it can ever get, and today was our day.

Everything seemed to have changed, and I felt as if I was on top of the world. I wondered how it would have been if Mummy had been there as I dressed as a bride that day, what she would have said, if she would have been happy to see me start a new phase of my life or felt sad that I was no longer going to be her little daughter. Dressing, which had lost its significance for me years ago, became of great importance on that day. I wanted so much to look beautiful that day—and make Vikas fall in love with me all over again!

The temple where we were to be wed smelt of marigold. Surrounded by our relatives, Vikas and I caught our first glimpse of each other as bride and groom. Vikas was dressed in a white cotton kurta pajama, while I wore an onion-pink georgette salwar kameez with ornate gold embroidery on it. This was the first time in all these years that I saw Vikas wearing Indian dress (he lived his life in jeans), and it suited him well. Our faces were radiant with happiness. We exchanged a smile. Vikas winked at me from across the hall and, as always, I blushed. Vikas often winked as a sign of appreciation when we were in a crowd. The wink was his way of communicating his approval to me. In the past, it had happened when I was with media people at a shoot for a television programme, at a press conference or on stage receiving an award. His wink was worth more than a thousand words.

We sat in front of the ritual fire taking our vows. Both of us felt tremendous contentment. It had been a long journey for us to reach here, but that journey had been as beautiful as each moment of the ceremony. When I look back and think of that day, I still find it hard to believe that it really happened. It could not have been more perfect.

We had very carefully, in advance, detailed each step of the ceremony to ensure that everything moved smoothly, without my disability becoming an awkward issue anywhere. Our preparations worked well. I did not drive my electric wheelchair over anyone's toes, nor did Vikas let my hand out of his while walking around the fire during our pheras. Everything went smoothly, and we were married. Unbelievable but true, we were husband and wife now! It sank in when everyone present rushed to us immediately and after endlessly hugging relatives, touching their feet, shaking hands and thanking people for their wishes and countless group photographs clicked with everyone.

Daddy and Meera, in the last two days of the celebration, had managed to get past whatever was in their hearts to bless Vikas and me as we started our life together. But the person I wanted the most to be there, blessing us, was Mummy. I could imagine her hugging us with tears of joy in her eyes and requesting Vikas to take care of her daughter through good and bad times. I really missed hugging her tightly as I cried tears of joy and apprehension about starting my new life, hoping that I would be as good a wife and daughter-in-law as Mummy had been. I knew she was present on this big day, overseeing that everything happened right. I knew we had her blessings.

The wedding concluded late. By the time we reached the reception venue after changing our clothes, there were over 200 people waiting for us. The evening at the Garden of Five Senses was magical. The weather was salubrious, and the garden had been decorated beautifully with lights accentuating its sculptures, fountains and trees. There was a stage for us to sit on with a ramp for me. The rest of the venue was accessible too. A throne-like seat had been put there for Vikas; I continued to sit on my motorized wheelchair next to him. There seemed to be a never-ending queue of well-wishers who came up to us one by one, congratulating us, handing over their gifts and getting a photograph clicked with the bride and groom. Ira and Ram, my adorable niece and nephew, ran up and down the stage the entire evening, collecting the innumerable gifts and flowers that we received and placing them all together on a table. While our smiles slowly became rather plastic after three hours of receiving guests, the kids' vigour did not recede.

The vibes at the venue were like none I had felt before at a wedding, probably because it was mine. Everyone was happy and enjoyed themselves, and it seemed that the evening had been orchestrated by angels. It was the most beautiful day of our lives and would remain etched in our hearts forever.

It was about 3 a.m. by the time we were finally alone in our hotel room, specially decorated and organized for us by an old friend. We toasted our love with champagne, still unable to believe that we were really wed. It was when Vikas took me in his arms—looking into my eyes and saying, 'So, Mrs

Sharma, how does it feel?'—that it seemed to seep in. It was the most beautiful moment of the entire day. We had been together countless times, but the truthfulness of that moment was worth more than anything else in my entire life.

꙰

There is nothing that could have prepared me for marriage. I doubt if I really knew what marriage meant even at the age of thirty-nine. To understand marriage, I think, one needs to really experience it. In my case, I was at a disadvantage because I had never given marriage a deeper thought as I had been sure it wouldn't be for me; moreover, I had had no opportunity to think of the change it would bring since I had been absorbed in all the preparations. But now that I was married, it completely changed me and I was happy with that change. Marriage also changed the world's expectations of me. From someone who was appreciated for managing her own life, I was now expected to be the heart of my family. I had thought that marriage was the end goal for our long relationship, but it turned out to be a beginning.

I had believed that my life was spun around Vikas's, with him being the most important person for me; but now it seemed that I had not known what spun around meant. I was changing because I wanted Vikas to be happy, as all that mattered to me, more than ever now, was him. There were a lot of adjustments both of us needed to make. From free-spirited lovers, we had become a tied-down married couple. Suddenly, what people thought about us seemed important, and this importance manifested itself in different ways.

After all these years, Vikas suddenly wanted me to become

more independent. This feeling, I believe, was an outcome of his concern about how his family would perceive me, to make me fit in with the general perception of a wife as being someone who could manage several things with ease. He also wanted me to start preparing myself for living together with his parents—a big step considering I had lived on my own for so long. But I was willing to give everything a chance and was open to all the changes. I wanted to fit into this new family.

Being married, I was expected to dress up. I had expected this and had purchased some ethnic clothes to wear when we were invited to family dinners. Vikas dressed me up each time we went out, something he had never been bothered about before. It mattered to him that I, his wife, looked presentable to his family. He helped me decide on my outfit, helped me put on my jewellery, my bindi, and so on. Getting ready for the occasion was the part I cherished more than the actual going out. I loved all the attention I was getting from Vikas.

Vikas moved into my house after our wedding. Since Vikas's parents lived on the first floor, it was easier that they come over to our house instead of us going to them. Vikas was very happy to have both his parents and me in his life together; so were his parents. They came over often to have dinner with us. There was happiness and love all around, and our evenings together were always warm and enjoyable.

I missed Daddy, though. Vikas and Daddy had not got off to a good start, but I was sure that the two most important men in my life would come around sometime, and I had no option but to just wait.

Vikas's two years in India were getting over soon and he was planning to take up a job in the UK. I was to join him for a few months once he was settled there.

Just a month after our wedding was Vikas's birthday. He was keen to celebrate it with his extended family once again, after ten whole years. We invited all the people he wanted to share this day with to our house for dinner, about twenty family members. It was the first time in my life that I hosted a party for family as I had always had only friends over for parties. With friends, one is carefree; but with Vikas's relatives coming to our house for the first time, everything had to be perfect. I was nervous, Vikas was excited. It seemed like a little test to me. A test that, if we passed, would put the family at ease and remove all doubts about how happy and comfortable Vikas was. His family was aware that it was only because he was now married to me that they had him back.

There was gaiety all the way that evening. Together, we had far beyond what we had dreamt of. I passed the test, and everybody was convinced Vikas was happy. I finally had a family, something I had longed for all my life.

27

Time was flying. It was already a few months since we had been married and it was soon going to be time for Vikas to return to the UK. Therefore we started planning for our first family holiday with his parents, something his father had been especially looking forward to since he had very recently retired from his job as a magistrate. It was decided that we would go to Manali for the long weekend holiday, and all the bookings were made. We were going to leave on 13 August 2009, exactly four months after our wedding. I was looking forward to it more because I hoped to bond better with Vikas's parents.

The morning we had to leave, unfortunately, we had a bad start. Ritu announced that she was leaving her job right then for no apparent reason. I was frantic. The house was in a mess after the monthly groceries shopping I had done at the super market the previous day, the plants needed to be watered, none of us had had breakfast yet, we hadn't packed for the trip. In the middle of all this chaos, this announcement unnerved me greatly. But the most important question was: who would look after Ubbu while we went to Manali if Ritu left?

I came wheeling to the living room, where Vikas was sitting at the dining table and setting an out-of-office auto responder for both of us. I sat next to him with my elbow resting on the table and my head on my palm, and said, 'What are we going to do now? Ritu is leaving.'

With a calm smile on his face, Vikas just sat there in his shorts and T-shirt, a cigarette in his hand. He said coolly, 'Just relax! Let her go. We'll work something out.'

'Gosh, how can you ask me to relax? What are we going to do?' I said frantically. This was a trip that we had been planning for a month. Vikas's mother had made the arrangements for our stay. After breaking the fourteen-hour journey to Manali in Chandigarh, we would stay three days and nights in Manali. I didn't want to be the spoilsport, the person upsetting the programme. In spite of being exhausted from our recent travels to Pune and southern India for work and running a fever, there was no way I was going to drop out. But things seemed out of control now. I felt very tense.

'Where are we going to leave Ubbu?' I asked. 'Daddy is not in Faridabad at the moment, otherwise we could have left her with him.' I was going mad. 'What are we going to do?' I kept repeating.

Ritu left after packing her bags. Things were slipping out of my hands.

Vikas picked up the yellow pages and called a pet boarding facility. They asked him what kind of a dog we had. 'Is it a pure breed or a mixed breed?' Ubbu was a mix, so they said: 'Sorry, we don't keep mixed breeds. They cry a lot after their master leaves and it disturbs the other dogs.' So that was no help.

Vikas then called another boarding facility. They were happy to keep any dog and it was very inexpensive, but the catch was they were going to keep the dog in a cage.

'Ubbu live in a cage?' I said with deep concern.

Vikas turned towards me and looked into my eyes. 'You're not happy with that, are you?'

Ubbu, born mid-February, was our Valentine baby. Neither of us could dream of leaving her in a boarding facility where she would be caged while we made merry in Manali.

Just then, the doorbell rang. Our driver, Lalit, was at the door. I had asked him to come today as I wanted him to clean the car before we started the journey. He wanted the car keys. Without a thought, I gave him the keys, not even sure if we would make the journey at all now. I wheeled back to Vikas, who was calling another boarding service. They too kept dogs in a cage. It was becoming clear now that a boarding service was not the answer. We had to think of something else.

Suddenly, I got a brainwave. I asked Lalit if he could stay four nights in my house, taking care of Ubbu. Lalit had been working for us for only five months now, but I was comfortable with leaving the whole house to him. He had been there with me during all the wedding running around and had proved to be hardworking and honest. Throughout the wedding functions, he acted as a family member rather than just a driver, working till late in the night, managing chores and last-minute goof ups. At my wedding, he single-handedly took the responsibility of carting my humongous motorized wheelchair from home to the two venues and ensuring that it was fully charged at all times. Now, to put me at ease, he agreed to stay and look after Ubbu.

And so it was all settled. I was really relieved. But as I said, it was a bad morning, as though everything was stopping us from going. Ubbu now started behaving peculiarly. She started getting into my wheelchair, not allowing me to move, and whined if I shooed her. This was very strange behaviour for her. She clearly didn't want us to go. She tried her best to stop us, but I just couldn't understand what she was trying to communicate, nor did I have the patience to listen to her wordless complaints since we were already running late. Enabling her to stay in her own environment while we were gone was the best I could do for. She continued to whine. I tried consoling her but it was useless, so we just ignored her and started getting ready.

By the time we picked up Vikas's parents and were finally on our way, we were three hours behind schedule. Thankfully, we were staying the first night in Chandigarh, which was a five-hour drive from Delhi. We stayed at a guesthouse after we reached around 8 p.m. Vikas and I were given a room on the ground floor, while his parents were on the first floor. All of us were exhausted after the long day and ordered dinner in our rooms. We decided to leave early for Manali as it was going to be another nine or ten hours of driving. We slept early and deep, unaware of what fate had in store for us the next day.

28

Control seems an illusion—
all I do is live my destiny,
happy or sad is up to me.
Possession seems an illusion,
as everyone was born free
To live their own destiny.

I can't forget the last time Vikas and I looked into each other's eyes. It was right after the car accident on our way to Manali.

We were about three hours short of Manali when an oil tanker hit us head-on. It was around two-thirty in the afternoon. Vikas struggled to avoid the collision, but he couldn't. In that instant, everything seemed to move in slow motion. Vikas and I looked at each other, aware of the inevitable... Then a crash that pushed our car perpendicular to the road... The next moment, we were still looking at each other, with my head on the dashboard and his on the steering wheel.

Blood was oozing from Vikas's chin and from my neck as we stared into each other's eyes. It was probably just a few seconds, but it seemed like a lifetime. So much was communicated through that look... *Thank God you are alive! Don't worry, everything will be fine. I am with you always...*

The moment was shattered as people came running from all sides to get us out of the car. People we didn't know. I struggled to speak—I wanted them to help Vikas first—but my words were drowned by an asthma attack that I could feel surging up in my chest. My seat belt was cut off, and I fell out of the car. In a daze I realized that strangers were carrying me to the side of the road. The village women had surrounded me and were assuring me again and again that everyone was fine.

I could not speak at all because of the magnitude of the asthma attack. Lying on the side of the road, I gestured at the village women for my purse. They understood and got it for me. I must have shocked many who misunderstood this as my desire to have my money safe in the midst of such a crisis. I asked the women helping me to open the purse. When I tried to pull out my inhaler, I realized that my hand hurt a lot. Somehow I managed to take a few puffs of the wonder drug recommended by our hosts in Panchgani just a week ago. As I look back, I wonder if I averted an exit from this life by taking the drug. In retrospect, I am not entirely happy that I did.

With the asthma under control, I looked around. The car was badly damaged. Vikas's mother was carried out and laid down next to me. Her face was bloody and her eyes were closed. I lost myself for a moment. All I could say was: 'Is she breathing?' The village women assured me that she was. In the background, I could hear words like 'neck hurt'. I didn't know who they were talking about, nor had the presence of mind then to comprehend what was being said. It was all like a dream yet very real. It almost felt as if I was looking at the situation through somebody else's eyes, as if I wasn't the main character in my own life. Instead, it was the people flocking around who appeared to be in control.

Passing cars were stopped to transport us to the nearest hospital in Mandi. I was bundled into someone's brand new

Scorpio, in the backseat, with my legs stretched out. It was then that I realized I had a broken leg. Above the knee, my right leg seemed to be attached to the rest of my body by just a little muscle. A ring of blood around the injury showed through my pink track pants.

I had started the journey dressed in track pants and a full-sleeved T-shirt. Papaji, which is how I had started addressing Vikas's father (and his mother was Mummyji), had laughed at me for being all dressed up to face Manali's cold from Delhi itself. I had laughed too, but had decided that I would be better off being warmly clad, considering that the impact of the car's AC would be more in the front seat. Despite this, after the accident I shivered uncontrollably for a long time.

On reaching the hospital, the occupants of the car could not figure out how to take me out, not wanting to further damage my leg. Finally, a few men came along, carried me out and put me on a stretcher. Through all this, I thanked the car owner and apologized for staining his seat with blood. Fortunately, the plastic covers of the car seats had not been removed, so cleaning up would not be all that difficult.

The hospital staff took us in reluctantly. 'Another accident case!' were words that I could hear all around. This was, by far, the most ill-equipped hospital I had ever seen and looked more like a hostel than a hospital. I was moved to an empty ward. Soon after, a stretcher with Papaji was brought into the ward and placed on the floor some distance away from me. I could see him clearly. His chest was bare. A lady doctor came in and checked his still body. Then she pronounced him dead.

My head reeled. Everything around me seemed surreal and I felt numb. I wondered where Vikas and Mummyji were being taken. All I hoped for was their wellbeing.

Next, an inspector came and asked me whom he should inform about the accident. I saw my mobile in his hand and asked for it. As luck would have it, the battery had run out and my mobile was off. I panicked as I did not remember any numbers besides my home one and my father's mobile. There was no point calling my father since he was not in Delhi. Then I remembered that my driver, Lalit, would be at home taking care of Ubbu. I called Lalit and told him to let Asha Bua know about our accident and tell her to inform Vikas's uncle.

The daze had taken over all my senses. There was no understanding of time, pain or loss. Life seemed completely out of control. Our education, our social status, our material possessions had no meaning at that moment. The situation had taken charge, and my family and I lay there helpless. There was a flurry of onlookers, helpers, inspectors and doctors, and there was nothing that we could do.

Within what seemed like half an hour, we were shifted again—this time all in one ambulance. Vikas was on the top; Papaji and Mummyji were at the bottom on either sides of the ambulance. There was barely space for another stretcher, so mine was precariously placed in between Papaji and Mummyji. The only sound to be heard through the entire journey was Mummyji snoring, and that was a great source of solace to me. We were being taken to a hospital in Sundernagar. All this made little sense to me. Sundernagar and Mandi were merely signboards that we had spotted while driving up.

On reaching the Sundernagar hospital, Vikas, Mummyji and I were taken to one of the wards. Vikas looked active and in his senses. He was the one talking to the inspector and to relatives on the phone. He was in charge in spite of all his injuries. I could hear him telling the doctor that I was a tetraplegic from an earlier accident. Vikas and Mummyji's wounds were stapled. The nurse asked the doctor to staple my neck too. I pulled my shoulder up so that my injury would not show—the thought of stitches on my neck was very scary. By now I was aware that Vikas too had a broken femur, but I was hoping that it was not as bad as mine.

In the meantime, the police had been through all our belongings and put together all the cash and other valuables like cameras and mobiles. I also heard them talking to some relative on the phone and informing them about the accident and telling them that two women and one man were alive. Magistrate Sahib was no more.

The next thing I remember was being taken to an ambulance yet again. This was probably after another half an hour. I was put into an omni ambulance, while Vikas and Mummyji were put into a larger ambulance. Papaji's body was being retained in Sundernagar.

There was a man with me in the van. He told me that we were been taken to the PGI Hospital in Chandigarh. The word Chandigarh was all that I understood, and instantly thought of Sunita Didi, my cousin who lived there. I was still stunned. I was also scared and lonely. I remember holding the strange man's hand for most of the journey to feel the reassurance of human touch. When I think back, I realize that I must have slept through most of the journey. I remember answering a couple of phone calls and enquiring about Vikas constantly.

It was sometime during this ride that Jiya called and talked to me. It was her voice that made me burst out in the tears that I had been holding back till now. Crying, I said to her, 'Why me? Why am I never given an option of if I want to continue living or not? Why does this happen to me again and again?'

We reached Chandigarh around 9 p.m. It was dark and wet from the rain. As soon as my ambulance door opened, I saw Arvind—Sunita Didi's husband, and a familiar face—and felt a sense of hope that things would be fine from here onwards.

The PGI Hospital, supposedly the pride of Chandigarh and the best hospital in that region, was a shameful looking place with dreadful services and inadequate resources. The emergency ward was full of patients, and their families all circled one junior doctor who seemed to be holding fort alone. Thoughts of that day when I was lying on a stretcher in the AIIMS corridor returned—AIIMS too had been full of patients waiting for admission, and as underequipped as PGI. This hospital, however, was worse—the stretcher I was transferred to from the ambulance was soaking wet from the rain.

Vikas and I lay on stretchers while Mummyji, who was still unconscious, was transferred to a bed. Vikas, whose stretcher was right in front of me, was the most aware of us and was complaining of a stomach ache. Thankfully, the doctor was reviewing Vikas with concentration. They did an ultrasound for Vikas and detected internal bleeding in his stomach. Mummyji became conscious for a short while and walked to the toilet, which was a good sign. She was diagnosed with a head injury and a fracture in the right arm. I had a broken femur, a fractured left hand and a deep gash across my neck, but I didn't need a doctor to tell me this.

Our relatives from Delhi reached the hospital soon. After initial examinations, the doctors said that Mummyji and I could be shifted to Delhi if we wanted, but Vikas had to stay back. Because of the bleeding in his stomach, shifting him was not recommended.

Everyone was in a state of shock, so we agreed to whatever the doctors said. Mummyji and I were shifted to Delhi while Vikas stayed back in that horrible hospital, with Mamaji staying back to look after him. I was uncomfortable moving to Delhi without Vikas, but there was absolutely nothing I could do. I could barely think straight, leave alone take any decisions. Mamaji assured me that he'd get Vikas to Delhi as soon as the doctors gave permission.

We were brought straight to a super speciality hospital in Delhi in an ambulance. Mummyji had not regained full consciousness yet. More family was waiting for us at the emergency of unit this hospital. Jiya too had reached Delhi by now and was there to receive us when we reached.

Seeing Dr Bajaj, someone I had known for years now, put me at ease. I had been shivering since the time of the accident, nearly twenty-four hours ago now. 'Shivani, what can I do for you?' Dr Bajaj asked me. This was the most reassuring moment for me in a long time. I was happy that he asked me what was it that I needed instead of taking over and dictating to his team about what to administer.

I said softly, my voice weak, 'I'm feeling very cold and I think you need to amputate my leg.' The doctor smiled and asked the nurses to immediately get a blower and a thermal blanket and to remove my wet clothes. The nurses obeyed the doctor's orders efficiently. My clothes were cut off as I could not be lifted to remove them. Once again, memories of my first accident returned. However, within a few minutes, I fell off to sleep because, surrounded by familiar faces and doctors I knew, I now felt safe.

When I woke up, I was groggy. Drips were attached to my body. In front of me was a college friend I hadn't met for twenty years. 'Where am I? What are you doing here?' My friend told me that I was in the ICU and had already been operated on. It was apparently early morning the next day and he had come to meet me after hearing about the accident. Both Mummyji and I had been operated on; she lay on the bed next to me, still unconscious. She stayed so the whole week because of her head injuries.

Mummyji and I were shifted the same day to a two-bedded ward room, where we lay next to each other for a week. The room was always flooded visitors, members from our families and friends and acquaintances. Everyone was horrified by our accident. Mummyji was not told about Papaji because of her own condition. She was discharged a day before me, still not fully aware of the situation.

While we were been taken care of in Delhi, Vikas was still in that dreadful hospital in Chandigarh. The day we got admitted to the hospital had been 14 August 2009. The next day was Independence Day, a national holiday. The doctors told Mamaji that there was good news, that Vikas's internal bleeding would be managed by oral medicine. Mamaji called and passed on the information to everyone in Delhi. In the middle the horror that we were going through, this was good news and made all of us happy. None of us realized that this was the worst news we could get. The only reason the doctors had put him on oral medication was because they were not in the mood to operate on him on their holiday.

Vikas was operated on the day after, on 16 August—a day late because of doctors' negligence. Jiya and my cousin Toto left for Chandigarh to be with Vikas and also to relieve Mamaji, who had been battling alone was by now exhausted.

PGI was supposed to be the best government hospital in that

region. Yet, just like at AIIMS, their nursing care was dismal. Pre- and post-operation, Vikas never got an allocation in the ICU even as his condition deteriorated. He just lay there on a bed, fighting hard to recover and return to us. He was not ready to leave us. He was put on a ventilator after the surgery and kept sedated. Just as they had lied to me years ago, doctors kept reassuring us that he would be fine, never disclosing the seriousness of the situation until it was completely out of hand.

Even today, when I look back, I regret that we did not have Vikas airlifted to Delhi. But everybody was in a state of shock and going by the Chandigarh doctors' advice; independent thinking was simply beyond us. And thus we were at the mercy of a bunch of heartless people for whom life had little meaning. Once again, it was the negligence of doctors that took everything away from me.

While our hospital room was full of familiar faces, Vikas was alone in that rotten government hospital with only Jiya, Toto (whom he had met only thrice before) and a couple of Vishal's friends for company. Vishal wanted to be with Vikas, but he was delayed by two days as he had to complete the last rites for Papaji.

After fighting to get better for a full week, Vikas finally gave up when he developed septicaemia that resulted in multiple organ failure. He was thirty-three years old.

29

Vikas was dead. An incomprehensible reality.

I was to be discharged from hospital on the same day. I would be attending the cremation before going home, the same home that a little more than a week ago had been alive with the excitement of planning our first family trip.

I had not been able to sleep for the past two nights. Each time I closed my eyes, I was woken up by thoughts and images that I could not make any sense of. The doctors thought it was a side effect of all the medication I was taking, but I know now it wasn't so. It was a premonition of the future that lay ahead. It was as though, somewhere in my soul, I knew what was coming, in spite of Jiya and Toto promising me that they would get Vikas to Delhi alive and recovering.

The news came at the break of dawn. My aunts and uncle were there at the hospital early to tell me about it. But before they could say anything, I already knew. I could read it in their faces and in their nervousness. Yet, the words hit me like a 1,000-watt jolt. 'Vikas is no more.'

I lay on the hospital bed, disbelieving tears rolling down my cheeks. I consoled myself by saying 'Everything will be fine. It will all work out right.' I was sure that Vikas would come back. After all, he had always done so for ten years. I quietly waited for Jiya to return from Chandigarh and tell me that everything was going to be just fine.

Within two hours, as the news spread, people started visiting me in the hospital to convey their condolences. The guards had been told of the tragedy and instructed not to stop any people coming to my room. It was all so bizarre and unreal. I felt like I was a part of some drama—someone else's drama. While at one level I knew why they were visiting, at another level I couldn't get myself to believe what had happened. 'Vikas can't leave. He promised to be with me when I grew old—when my hair turned grey and my teeth fell out,' I kept telling myself. My eyes moistened each time a visitor walked in, but I could not find my voice to say anything. A friend came and stood next to me and said, 'Now what good can there be in this!' Her words were loud and jarring to my ears. Friends surrounded me, yet I had never felt so alone ever before.

It was close to afternoon when Jiya and Toto reached the hospital. Toto hugged me, weeping inconsolably and apologizing profusely for not being able to keep his promise. Of course it was not his fault, but the guilt of not having kept his promise was gnawing at him. Both Jiya and Toto had toiled day and night to get Vikas better, much more than anyone else could have done. But what had to be had to be…

Surrounded by family and friends, I found myself overcome by a feeling of drowning in a strange nothingness, as though there was nothing that mattered any longer.

Preparations for taking me to the cremation ground started. I needed clothes other than the hospital clothes, and a vehicle to take me there as I still bed-bound and could not travel in a regular vehicle with my fractured leg. Jiya told me that everything was being organized. A nightgown had been arranged for and an ambulance was on its way to take me. With a faint smile on my face, I said softly, almost muttering to myself, 'Vikas hated me in nightgowns.'

As the time to go to the ground drew closer, I started shivering. My friends tried to calm me and coax me into eating something to have strength for the cremation. But, of course, I was unable to comprehend anything. Only nothingness prevailed.

'We need to leave in half an hour, Chots, you better get ready,' Jiya said. My friends helped me out of the hospital clothes and into a pair of trousers that somehow went around the leg brace, and a T-shirt. Jiya had made sure that I was not wearing the hated nightgown as I accompanied Vikas on his last journey.

By the time my ambulance reached the cremation ground after navigating through Delhi's traffic, the ceremony had nearly ended. Hundreds of people were gathered there, waiting for me to come and take my last look at Vikas. He lay absolutely still, covered in a white sheet. I was terrified to my bones. I had been unsure about seeing Vikas now that he was gone, fearing that the last memory of his closed eyes would stay with me forever. But he looked very peaceful, almost like an angel, with a smile on his face. I was instantly reminded of the times he had laughingly said that he was going to die early in his life, in a car accident, and then come back as a ghost. I told everyone around me about it. 'He will come back as an angel, not a ghost,' they said. 'Ghost or angel, how does it matter?' I thought, 'He will come back, and that is all that matters.'

Vikas's plinth was soon carried to the bed of wood. Everyone present went forward and placed a log atop his body. Soon it was set on fire. If only I could walk, I would have gone too. I wanted so much to embrace Vikas and just lie there with him. Instead, I lay silent on my stretcher, far away from him.

Mummyji cried hysterically. Just the day before, Vishal had informed her about Papaji's death and told her that Vikas was recovering...and today this. She came and hugged me tight, telling me that she would take care of me as I was 'a part of Vikas'.

Book 5

Another Journey

30

The only thing I believe in is love.
The only faith I have is that it will never abandon me.

I was brought home in the ambulance after the cremation ceremony. I asked to be settled on the bed in the guest room as the thought of going to the room I had shared with Vikas was unnerving. Also, my injuries could be cared for better on the single bed in the guest room.

I was glad to see Ubbu after so many days. The day we had left Delhi, Ubbu had tried to stop us frantically; not understanding her wordless language, we had left anyway. And now she wanted to sit by me and share my sorrow. She was allowed to do so but under vigilance as one had to make sure that she did not jump on my injuries. She climbed up carefully on the bed, sniffed at the casts on my leg and hand, and then left the bed and settled in one corner of the house. After that, she never tried climbing on my bed unless I invited her to do so.

Ubbu remained withdrawn for months, not barking at anybody despite the constant stream of visitors who came to condole. It was as if she had been infected by a bit of the sense of nothingness from me. Over time, however, she once again began to plug my emotional void. My baby grew up and began taking care of me, making sure I got up in the mornings and not letting me drown myself in grief. She gave me reason to smile, showing me that all was not over. I could probably not have managed to go on without her.

Ritu did not speak a word when I reached home. She had returned after she heard the news, and now immersed herself in making me comfortable. No one else understood how she had been a witness to and shared moments of our togetherness for eight years. She mourned not only my loss but also for herself—Vikas had been like a big brother to her. She stayed up all night, nursing me through the delirious condition that I was in for countless days. Nights were the most frightening, when I found myself haunted by meaningless dreams. Throughout the night, my mouth and throat kept drying up; Ritu would keep giving me sips of water, mumbling strange things.

My family stayed with me to take care of me. Lots of people kept coming by to condole. But I just lay silent on my bed, motionless and thoughtless, for a very long time. I was void of any desire or hope. I had no idea about how was I supposed to continue living. There was nothing for me to continue living for, not even kids. How was I supposed to go on? People said that this was the span of time Vikas and I had meant to be together. But how could that be, I wondered. Vikas had promised never to leave me, and he never broke any promise he made to me.

Everyone was very worried about me. They tried to divert my attention to thinking about AccessAbility. To continue Vikas's dream, I tried sincerely. A meeting was held at my house with Jiya, all my cousins and friends who were keen to support me to move forward. There were a lot of discussions about things I thought Vikas had wanted to do, but whether they were his dreams I did not know. A person like him could not have such small dreams. These were things that we had thought of doing together at AccessAbility, but life was far more than that. Finally, I realized that I needed to wind up the infrastructure as it was not going to be required anytime soon.

Time had lost significance and did not seem to move. I groped in the dark, searching for answers. I had already lived up to the challenges that life had once put to me and come out victorious. Then why was I required to do this all over again? It just didn't make any sense. I was someone who had the strength to rise to any challenge, I knew, but now there seemed to be no reason at all to rise again. After all, Vikas had had so many achievements, talents, ideas and plans, but everything had changed in an instant. I no longer saw any meaning or purpose in my work, the accolades, awards and media coverage I had received. It was all so hollow and transient.

For a while, I was very angry with God—whoever that was. I felt that God had pulled me out of a crowd and kicked me hard like a football. I lay in my bed thinking why it was always me having to rediscover myself again and again. Why was I the one who received these wild blows of fate just as I seemed to be getting comfortable in my life?

Days became weeks. Weeks became months. But nothing changed. As I lay in bed for eight months, recovering from my injuries, two questions plagued me. What is life? Why do I live?

Gradually, I started thinking about the dreams Vikas and I had shared. The only dream I had had was to be with Vikas; it was Vikas who had had countless dreams for me—to be the best professional, an inspirational person, independent and strong. It was he who would scan newspapers and stay up till

3 a.m. just to record a programme with me on TV. Because it was I who was his dream.

※

As time passed, my search for answers drew me to my inner self. It became easier for me to see my life objectively, with a degree of detachment. It was not hard for me to meditate as the lack of any desire had erased all the clutter from my mind. I came to the realization that, in the midst of all that was fleeting, a higher search and a deeper connection with oneself were the only things that held any real meaning. I felt calm and cleansed, like a slate that has been wiped clean.

Night, which had been frightening, became the best time of the day because of the silence that came with it. I was able to think most clearly then. I remained awake through countless nights, searching my soul and trying to get to know myself better. The only thought that presented itself to me was: 'In life, only love is a reality, and the only certainty is death.'

I was reminded that love is not about possessing but about letting go. It was as though Vikas were asking me to let go of his physical form and reassuring me that he would never leave me, and that I needed to continue with life because I was his dream. Long-ago heard words came back to me: 'Love is the most selfless feeling one can have; in fact, it is love only if it is selfless.' Therefore holding on to Vikas, just because I felt empty and lonely without him, was a selfish act. I had to allow him to be free.

There is a saying that true love never abandons you. Vikas, even if he was not physically present any longer, would never leave my heart. But I would find him only if I tried to rise from my grief and self-pity.

It was my search to find Vikas that made me see the purity of love as being unparalleled. I was sure beyond doubt that, in time, we would share another fascinating life together.

Death, a word so dreaded by all, was what actually gave me the meaning of life. Life and death, I understood, were inseparable from each other. One existed because of the other. Like joy and sorrow, happiness and pain, Vikas and Shivani.

In understanding this, I also understood that joy had made me complacent, whereas sorrow made me exert myself to improve further. I wondered why the feeling of happiness was so wonderful when it didn't help in self-growth—it is only in sorrow that one has the opportunity to bring about change.

All the pursuits I had been so involved in till now were ones in which I had had no space for real growth. I had felt like the biggest pauper without Vikas, as if everything had been snatched from me; but perhaps in the game of life I was at my richest, with this opportunity to understand life and death.

Until now, I had lived my life in pursuit of greater social recognition, striving hard to have the best education, acclaim for my work and a comfortable lifestyle. But, in a split-second, all of this had become meaningless, and all that mattered and remained was love. All these years I had felt bad about my failures. But now the word failure had no meaning—it was just as momentary as success. Understanding this gave me the strength to make a fresh start, but this time for love and not for worldly recognition. I could see just how simple life really was and how complex I had made it.

There was no way I could have arrived at this realization had it not been for the intense love I had shared with Vikas, and the nothingness that had been created by his death. I will be eternally indebted to Vikas, my soul mate, who through his life taught me to love, believe, accept, forgive and have gratitude, and in death he helped me understand life itself.

31

What I know from the life I lived
is that it's only love that's real.
Life for me has been a search for love,
through the cycle of life and death.
Life for me is about
having the belief that I'll find love,
having the courage to accept that love,
having the strength to lose that love,
rising again to find that love...
Because, in life, all that matters is love.

Even today, the intensity of my grief has not reduced, and I doubt if it ever will. People say that time is a healer, but with time I feel my sorrow increase.

There were many friends who were unable talk to me after the incident. I guess it is difficult for anyone to face sorrow and people want to stay away from it. And I wonder why sorrow is such a detested emotion. I had found peace in my sorrow, and the difference between happiness and sorrow seems to have disappeared. It is my sorrow that allows me internal growth and maturity. Yes, happiness does beget external prosperity, but it does not seem to touch the soul. I was immeasurably happy when we got married, but I was so complacent in that happiness that I had no time to think about it and appreciate it at a deeper level. Vikas's and my love for each other had always been intense, but I could not fathom it while we were happy together. It is only now, in sorrow, that I recognize that intensity, and the beauty of it. Besides, I am not eternal; sooner or later, I will be with Vikas again, and with a deeper understanding of our love.

It is sorrow that gives me the courage to listen to my heart instead of my head. It is easy to make decisions when you have nothing to lose. It is only now that I can see that all I ever had to lose was my love; but love is never lost, so in reality I never had anything to lose. It is only love that has any value; everything else is meaningless.

I believe that to love one requires a lot of courage. To make Vikas more important than myself was not an easy journey for me. I was a selfish person to begin with, looking only for a good time and a feeling of being desired by someone; all that had mattered to me was companionship to drive my loneliness away—it was all about me. But with Vikas, I grew and learnt the meaning of love. The only way to succeed in love is by shifting the focus from oneself to another. I had always thought I was able to do this far more easily than Vikas, but today I realize how much more Vikas had to give up to be with me. He stayed away from his family, he gave up all those friends who did not accept me. So many times, we were influenced by society and people around us in our expectations from each other; but Vikas was amazing at standing by his values and his principles, and he was willing to challenge the dogmatic attitudes exhibited towards disabled women in our society.

A friend wrote in a condolence note: 'You are the only person I know to have loved so deeply and got it back with the same intensity.' It is true. While it was in my hands to love deeply, to be loved in return with the same intensity was a blessing—and it is only now, in sorrow, that I recognize it.

Having learnt from Vikas to let love just flow freely, without inhibitions, today I am ready embark on a journey to redefine love once again—love as a reality that transcends physical form—by living a life he wanted and dreamt for me.

32

As I stepped out of my desolation, I could feel Vikas's presence everywhere. I could see him occupying his favourite chair, still the King of the Living Room. Not much had changed. The air still felt warm and smelt the same. The sun still lit the room through the window. The furniture was where it always was. Ubbu still sprawled on the floor, blocking the way for my wheelchair. When I looked around, I could see in flashes friends sitting around and making merry, Vikas's family over for dinners, Vikas sitting at the dining table with his laptop and working on improving our company website. I could hear the hip-hop music we so often played, hear me and Ritu discussing party menus, and Vikas telling us to keep our volume down as the entire world could hear us talk. And then I sat down at my round dining table, beside the kitchen door and facing the idiot box, typing out my life with one finger, the only one usable after the second accident.

Dressed in a shapeless nightgown, I sat in front of the computer every day—thinking, occasionally punching in a few pages, but mostly just thinking. Vikas's voice would sound in my ears: 'Miss Nightie, at least change your clothes. I hate seeing you in a nightgown.' My family was worried about me and for my future, but I knew from my experience that living life was not that difficult and knowing why you live was far more important.

Everyone was back in their lives, having gotten over the tragedy, but it was never going to be over for me. My life had changed forever. I had returned to AccessAbility, though I was not in full swing as yet. The thing holding me back was not the pain in my heart but the urge to document my life's journey. It would all be wasted if I were not able to reflect on it and really learn. The only thing that mattered was the book. I was writing to understand 'Why?' and to capture Vikas before time made everything dusty.

Just the thought of writing a book was somewhat unbelievable for me. I was the person whom everyone in office thought of as being dyslexic, fed up of my numerous spelling and grammatical errors. But writing was the only way I knew to bring Vikas to life again. I know that Vikas, wherever he was, did not believe me as I worked on my book, just like he hadn't when I told him I would be going to the UK for higher studies. It was my opportunity to prove myself to him once again, and for that I alone I was going to not give up on the challenge.

I could still see Vikas as my biggest critic, just as he was each time I emailed him lines to be edited. They would be returned within a minute with a note: 'I'm tired of cleaning up your shit. At least read what you have written ONCE before sending it to me.' Before I could even download and read the edited email, he would be standing behind me, leaning over my chair and saying: 'Just read what you have written!' Made nervous by his proximity, I would invariably read it as I thought I had written it instead of what I had actually written. 'You can't even read simple English! Which school are you from? Did they not teach you English?' Vikas would then scream. 'Welhams. It's the best girls' school in the country!' I would say meekly before continuing to try and read and edit my lines. This was a regular drill that occurred at least four times in a week. Everyone at work was used to us fighting over the pettiest of matters.

What had started as scribbles in old registers became the most revitalizing experience of my life. Not only did the journey of writing my book give me a chance to relive my entire life but it also gave me the opportunity to make sense of it all and let go of the negativity that blocked the clean flow of understanding. It gave me the courage to accept what fate had meted out to me and be strong enough to carry on.

The scribbles in the registers became pages on the computer as I refined the account of my life over and over again, trying to improve it by putting in deeper thoughts. I requested all my cousins and a few friends to give me feedback. As I progressed, I had to skip over many of the moments that to me were important but for a reader would be just too much information. I learnt to put in more emotion rather than just narrate things that had happened. The writing of the book became about redefining things again and again, and looking at my life from different perspectives.

I wondered what I would do if I had the power to go back and change anything in my past. Everything was so perfectly interwoven, with one event leading to another, for a reason. If I hadn't met Sunil, I would probably have not met with my first accident. But if I hadn't had my first accident, I would have never met Vikas. Without Vikas, I would not have found passion and love, and my life would have been meaningless

Perhaps I would have asked for Vikas to not go, but then that would have meant altering his journey...

As I relived my life, I could not help but appreciate the beauty of everything I had been fortunate enough to experience. After all, I had lived the life I wanted to, and not because someone else had wanted me to live it that way.

Epilogue

It is 13 April 2010. I am sitting peacefully, lost in the natural beauty of Leh, Ladakh. Just a few days ago, I dreamt that Vikas and I were celebrating our first wedding anniversary somewhere in the mountains, surrounded by snow. Being in Leh feels like déjà vu. I am here on a project for a travel company—to assist in creating an accessible travel package for disabled travellers. I am sure that it is Vikas who orchestrated my being here today. He had really wanted to visit Leh. In fact, we had had several fights wherein he accused me of not letting him go. My only excuse was that I too wanted to go with him.

It starts snowing gently as I sit in the balcony of my guesthouse room, looking at the snow-capped mountains. It is the perfect place to celebrate our anniversary.

I know that Vikas is here with me in spirit. I can almost see him sitting beside me, raising a toast to the magnificent life we have shared and counting all the blessings we have received. As I hear the clink of imaginary champagne flutes, tears roll down my eyes. I feel Vikas's embrace all around me. I whisper softly to him...

It has been so long
since I held your warm hand in mine,
heard your voice calling my name,

smelt the sweat on your body,
tasted your sweet lips.
Even today,
I feel you holding me,
telling me right from wrong,
demanding the most from me,
expecting the world from me,
making me feel real.

So long, my dear!
I hope you are happy and at peace,
as I struggle to find my peace,
trying to find meaning in this world...
You are the person who
gives me my sense of belonging,
the courage to face the world,
the untiring belief in myself
that compels me to go on.
And since I know I can't exist without you,
if I exist, then you exist too.

Acknowledgements

Writing a book was not something I had ever planned to do. It was circumstances that made it happen. It wouldn't have been written had it not been for my sister Gargi, who encouraged me to start writing a book in the darkest moments of my life.

I remember when in the middle of the night I would ask Ritu to give me my notebook to jot down the thoughts that flowed so clearly in the silence of the night. I would like to thank Ritu for her dedication and affection in supporting me in not only in writing my book but also in my pursuit to achieve all that I wish to.

I would like to thank all my family and friends, who constantly encouraged me and, in particular, Viraj, who patiently read the countless initial drafts.

I would like to thank Anuradha Goyal, a book critic I have never met, who just because of an email request read my initial draft and give me inputs on how to shape it into a book.

This book would not have been published without the support of Chitra Padmanabhan, who helped me improve the book and connected me with Rupa Publications.

I would like to thank Deepak Kirpalani (DK) for spending time to edit the book in spite of his extremely busy schedule.

I am thankful to Pradipta Sarkar from Rupa Publications for giving the book its final shape.

Finally, I would like to thank Vikas, my husband, without whom this book would not have been possible.

About the Author

Born on 23 December 1969, SHIVANI GUPTA is the founder of AccessAbility, and one of India's best-known access consultants. With degrees in inclusive environments (design and management), and diplomas in architecture technology and hotel management, Shivani has spent most of her professional life in working towards improving accessibility of public spaces such as educational institutions, hotels and retail and other commercial spaces in India. She has undertaken research on issues related to accessibility in India and contributed to policies for disabled persons in the country.

Apart from her work at the country level, Shivani has worked on international projects as a consultant with the Office of the United Nations High Commissioner for Human Rights, the International Disability Alliance, Disabled Peoples' International and the Christian Blind Mission. She has also co-authored three publications pertaining to improving accessibility in physical environments for disabled people.

Prior to becoming an accessibility consultant, Shivani worked as a peer counsellor with the Indian Spinal Injuries Centre, New Delhi; and a guest relations officer with the ITC Maurya Sheraton Hotel, New Delhi.

For her achievements in the disability sector, and her personal courage, Shivani has received national and international acclaim.

She has been honoured with the Helen Keller Award (2008), the CavinKare Ability Mastery Award (2008), the National Role Model Award (2004), the Neerja Bhanot Award (2004), the Red and White Social Bravery Award (1999), and the Sulabh International Woman of the Year Award (1996).

Shivani believes that there is nothing more disabling for persons with disabilities than society's failure to accept and include them as part of the mainstream. Her motto is 'Access = Ability'.